The Sacraments & You

The Sacraments & You
Living Encounters with Christ

Michael Pennock

Ave Maria Press • Notre Dame, Ind. 46556

Permissions and credits:

Excerpts from THE JERUSALEM BIBLE, copyright © 1966 by Darton, Longman & Todd, Ltd. and Doubleday & Company, Inc. Used by permission of the publisher.

Excerpts from the English translation of *Rite of Baptism for Children* © 1969, International Committee on English in the Liturgy, Inc. (ICEL); excerpts from the English translation of *Rite of Marriage* © 1969, ICEL; excerpts from the English translation of *Rite of Anointing and Pastoral Care of the Sick* © 1973, ICEL; excerpts from the English translation of *Rite of Penance* © 1974, ICEL; excerpts from the English translation of *Rite of Confirmation* © 1975, ICEL; excerpts from the English translation of *The Ordination of Deacons, Priests, and Bishops* © 1976, ICEL. All rights reserved.

Nihil Obstat:
      Rev. Mark A. DiNardo, Ph.D.
      Censor Deputatus

Imprimatur:
      Most Rev. Anthony M. Pilla, M.A.
      Bishop of Cleveland

Library of Congress Catalog Card Number: 81-65227
International Standard Book Number: 0-87793-221-2

Photography:
      Terry Barrett, cover, 148; Martinus Bombardier, cover, 212; Joseph M. Champlin, 182; Fred De Leu, cover; Vadim Dubinin, 156; J. Murray Elwood, 10, 19, 45; Rohn Engh, 96; Kay Freeman, 164, 247; Bruce Jennings, 110; Mary Ellen Kronstein, cover, 102; Jean-Claude LeJeune, 262; Tom McGuire, 34, 60, 68, 82; Carolyn A. McKeone, 134; Patrick Mooney, 52, 74, 172, 175, 188, 206; Notre Dame Printing & Publications Office, 222, 256; Sister Jane Pitz, 40; Anthony Rowland, 128; Bob Shirtz, 198; Paul Tucker, 242; Jim Whitmer, 94, 116, 140, 230, 239, 252.

Manufactured in the United States of America.

DEDICATION

One of the most satisfying definitions of the sacraments is that they are signs of God's love. I dedicate this book to two people who fit this definition well, my mother and father—Louise and Frank Pennock. They have been real signs of love to me, to their other children and grandchildren and to all who know them.

Acknowledgments

I wish here to thank all those wonderful people who have helped me in the writing of this book.

First, I want to thank my patient and loving wife Carol. She has supported all my work. Also, I wish to extend my gratitude to my four kids—all signs of God's love to Carol and me: Scotty, Jenny, Amy and our newest, Christopher.

Next, I wish to acknowledge the fantastic people at Ave Maria Press for encouraging me and supporting me in all my work. I am indeed privileged to have as my editor Frank Cunningham whose friendship and ideas are invaluable to me. Charlie Jones of Ave remains a constant source of encouragement as do Fr. Reedy, Gene Geissler and Joan Bellina.

Within the past year I received a Ph.D. from the University of Akron. I would especially like to thank my advisor Steve Thompson for his encouragement in my professional career. Other sources of inspiration at that institution are Hal Foster, Fred Schultz, Larry Bradley and Warren Kuehl.

Three men in particular have been my mentors over the years. Fr. Mark DiNardo is a source of support that is truly of the Lord. He gave me my initial impetus in writing and has encouraged me ever since. Fr. Paul Hritz taught me most of what I know. He is a great priest and a tremendous pastor. Dr. George Eppley is the kind of educator I aspire to be—creative and visionary. To all of them—thanks again.

Fr. Harry Fagan, pastor of Immaculate Conception Parish in Madison, Ohio, has continually valued me and my work. In return, I value his friendship and above all else his true Christian leadership.

Many teachers and friends have helped me make this a better book by their many suggestions and comments. The following especially deserve my gratitude: Marty Dybicz—a golfing buddy and a colleague whose friendship I treasure; Bert Polito—one of the finest young religious educators around; Jim Gutbrod—a seeker after the Lord; Paul Rodgers, S.J.—a dynamic teacher; Jim Finley—a friend and a leader in the field of catechetics.

I am one of those very lucky individuals who happen to teach at a great school with a great teaching staff. My principal Fr. Frank Cody, S.J., Ph.D., encourages my work and helps my teaching. His assistant Al Wilhelms has always been the best of administrators. Their concept of Christian ministry in a school is exemplary and supportive of those of us who labor for the Lord. My colleagues in the theology department are simply outstanding: Jim Skerl—my dynamic department chairman and incredible Christian witness to our students; Sr. Carolyn Capuano, H.M., who is one of my most trusted colleagues; Bert Polito, Marty Dybicz and Paul Rodgers, S.J.; Larry Belt, S.J., an outstanding Christian; Tom Ankenbrandt, S.J. whose sense of humor sustains us; and Ron Torina, S.J.—a man whose encouragement and affirmation have meant very much to me this past year or so. To all of you: thanks a lot.

Lastly, I once again want to affirm in this section of my book that my greatest source of inspiration and encouragement has always come from my students, the young men at St. Ignatius High School, Cleveland, Ohio. I have been most fortunate to teach them these past 11 years. I love each one of them (over 2,000). The following young men especially deserve my gratitude for their helpful and supportive comments on my original manuscript: Marc Spiros, Joe D'Alessandro, Paul Ferkul, Ken Peters, Pat Shields, Justin Smith, Jim Rossman, Geoff Miller, Joe McNamara and Dan Gaugler (who is also a golfing buddy!). These are all outstanding young men and represent the kind of people I have been privileged to teach over the years at Ignatius.

Special thanks to my friend Jeanette Kramer for typing my manuscript.

To all of you, to others who have loved and supported me over the years: Much thanks, God bless you and know that I love you all.

—Michael Francis Pennock

Contents

1

Sacraments—
Beginning with Jesus

I am the vine,
you are the branches.
Whoever remains in me, with me in him,
bears fruit in plenty;
for cut off from me you can do nothing.

—Jn 15:5

INTRODUCTION

This book is about the sacraments of Jesus. The sacraments are an important area of Christian life. They are a key way to meet our Risen Lord. Before we study the sacraments, however, we will take some time in this chapter to look at Jesus, his message and his importance for you as you grow in Christian faith.

Jesus is important. He himself claimed to be the beginning and the end. " 'I am the Alpha and the Omega,' says the Lord God, who is, who was, and who is to come, the almighty" (Rv 1:8). Anyone who claims this is worth listening to! Yet, we all know that so many times people ignore Jesus and what he has to offer us.

11

To illustrate the neglect Jesus has encountered, think of the 1970s. Some people called the '70s the "me decade." (It has never been called the "Jesus decade.") The "me decade" refers to the continuous search people undertook to find *personal* meaning. People were trying to find out how to be happy. Some took to drugs. Others read books on "How to be your own best friend" or "How to win through asserting yourself and putting others on the run." Still others entered "temporary commitments" with people so they would not be "too" hurt if the relationship fell apart. The focus in the "me decade" was on personal happiness; happiness which often failed to consider the welfare of others.

There is certainly nothing wrong with being happy or searching for personal meaning. There is nothing wrong with trying to find one's place in life. Pollsters tell us that young people, too, are caught up in the great search. The teen search seems to revolve around three issues: (1) What am I going to do in the future? (2) How do I look to others, that is, am I physically appealing? (3) What do members of the opposite sex think of me?

These are important concerns and the answers to them do help determine our happiness. The potential problem, though, is that in searching for the answers we might neglect other people. We might focus so much on our own problems and concerns that we shut out the love, the problems, the concerns of others in the same situation of groping for meaning in life.

What is tragic about the quest for personal happiness is that we might very well neglect the One who is the "beginning and end" of human life, the One who might very well be the key to happiness. Christians, of course, believe that Jesus is that One who provides the answer to our questions of meaning, that he is the way to happiness. If we are too "me-centered," we may not hear what he has to say, we may fail to see him standing at our side helping us work out our happiness.

With these thoughts in mind, let us pause for a bit in this chapter to see what Jesus has to say, to look at what he stands for, to reflect on how he can help us on our way to happiness.

REFLECTION AND DISCUSSION

1. Do you agree with the studies that claim young people are most concerned about: (1) their futures; (2) their looks; and (3) their appeal to members of the opposite sex? Why or why not? What other concerns would you add to the list?

2. Happiness is _____

_____.

3. *Happiness Quiz:* Check the item in each group of choices below which you think would make you happier.

A. ____ good looks   B. ____ happy family life
    ____ high intelligence   ____ success in the
                                      work world

C. ____ warm, comfort-   D. ____ good health
        able home   ____ superior athletic
    ____ fancy car with   ability
        plenty of gas
        money

E. ____ high-paying job F. ____ sexual attrac-
    ____ two or three   tiveness
        close friends   ____ ability to hold
                               onto a relation-
                               ship with a loved
                               one

G. ____ ability to play
        the piano
        money to travel
        far and wide

Share your choices with a classmate. Compare/contrast answers. Why did you choose as you did? How do you think Jesus would choose? Why?

At the end of his Gospel, the apostle John wrote, "There were many other things that Jesus did; if all were written down the world itself, I suppose, would not hold all the books that would have to be written" (Jn 21:25). John was pointing out that no summary of the deeds of Jesus can exhaust who he is, what he has done, what he means for us. With John's caution in mind, though, let's take a look at some of the high points about Jesus and his message. Along the way, we'll relate these to the sacraments. The following points will be discussed:

I. The centrality of the incarnation of Jesus.

II. Jesus' call to conversion.

III. The good news of forgiveness (reconciliation).

IV. Jesus' call to unity.

V. The message of love.

VI. Jesus as the message.

I. The Incarnation. What is meant by the Incarnation? Simply put, Christians believe that God became man in the person of Jesus Christ. Matthew said it well in his Gospel: "The virgin will conceive and give birth to a son, and they will call him Emmanuel (a name which means 'God is with us')" (Mt 1:23). God becoming man, entering human history as a fellow human, becoming flesh like us is the mystery of the Incarnation.

In a certain way, it makes no logical sense to say that the Almighty, the powerful God who created all, would so humble himself to become one of us. But this is the great truth of our faith: Jesus is God made man. Jesus is God with us.

The Incarnation, God becoming man, happened as a result of God's promise to be with his people. As you might well recall, this promise began with God's choosing a special people through the patriarch Abraham. The promise was renewed at the time of the Exodus when God led the poor ragtag slaves from Egypt, sustained them in the desert and then gave them their own land "flowing with milk and honey." The promise was renewed time and again through the trials and tribulations of the Jews, that is, through their sufferings, the collapse of their kingdom, their captivity by foreign powers, their unfaithfulness to their gracious God. The promise was always there.

And then he came. Not as a fancy king, but as a poor child honored first by the lowly shepherds (Lk 2:8-18). He grew up as we did, in age, in wisdom, in grace (Lk 2:52). He was like us in everything but sin (Heb 4:15). He lived his life as a youth hidden in a small town, the village of Nazareth, until he reached the age of 30 or so when he began his mission.

The Gospels say little about Jesus' youth because they are concerned about reporting his public life, his mission of salvation to the world. This public mission, as we know so well, consisted of teaching the people about his Father, of healing, of challenging people to be the children of God they were meant to be. This mission was done in the midst of ordinary life. Jesus walked dusty roads. He enjoyed meals with his friends. He spent a lot of time in the open air, praying in the hills, resting at the seashore, seeking people out in the marketplace. In other words, Jesus lived life to the full until he was ready to give up his life for the salvation of his friends, for all of mankind.

What are we to learn from this? Because *God* became one of us, in a certain sense we became God. Humans are no longer insignificant "nothings" in the cosmic scheme. We are brothers and sisters to God who became our brother. All of human life, all of created reality is holy. The food we eat, the clothes we wear, the games we play, the jokes we enjoy, the work we do, the rest we seek are all important to God who became one of us. This is the importance of the Incarnation. Because God became man, he showed us firsthand that everything connected to human life is worthy, is sacred, has meaning and importance. He shared in all of these realities. He was born; he died. He laughed; he cried. He worked. He was tempted. He was like us.

The first great lesson of Jesus is that we should take great comfort in the fact that we are vitally important to him, that the things that concern us concern him. Because he was one with us, what is important to us is important to him. What has meaning for us has meaning for him. In fact, the sacraments make just this point. God comes to us in a special way in the key events of our lives. He comes to us at birth and at death. He is there with the Spirit of his love to strengthen us as we grow. He feeds us together at the banquet table of his Eucharist. He stands ready to forgive us when we sin and are guilt-ridden. He sustains us in our vocations as married people or as ministers to his people. Because he is Emmanuel—God with us—he is a God who cares about everything that happens to us.

FOR FURTHER REFLECTION

1. Read the following key passages from the Old Testament. What connection do they have with the mystery of the Incarnation?

   a. 2 Sm 7—God's covenant with David

   b. Is 11—Sevenfold spirit of the Messiah

   c. Is 53—The Suffering Servant

   d. Ez 32—Promise of the Good Shepherd

   e. Dn 7—Vision of the Son of Man

2. Read Mt 6:26-34. Discuss what this passage means.

3. "As for you, every hair of your head has been counted; so do not be afraid of anything" (Mt 10: 30-31).

   Put an *X* next to any items that are presently of concern to you.

   ____ getting into college

   ____ getting along with my teachers

   ____ finding a job

   ____ winning a game

   ____ passing a test

   ____ planning the weekend

   ____ developing a close friendship with a member of the opposite sex

   ____ a problem with drugs or drinking

   ____ how I look to others

   ____ a friend in trouble

   ____ my relationship with my parents

   ____ what to do about my future career

   ____ owning a car

   ____ a bad habit

   ____ family not working

   ____ family member having a problem

List some other concerns here:

   a. _____

   b. _____

   c. _____

After completing this exercise, share it with a friend or classmate. Now, together read Lk 11:5-13. What is your attitude to this passage where Jesus speaks of prayer? Do you believe it? Would you like to believe it?

II. Call to Conversion. When Mark wrote his Gospel, he wasted no time getting to the heart of Jesus' mission:

> After John had been arrested, Jesus went into Galilee. There he proclaimed the Good News from God. "The time has come," he said, "and the kingdom of God is close at hand. Repent, and believe the Good News!"
>
> (Mk 1:14-15)

Jesus was acutely aware of the fact that he ushered in a new age. He realized that as his Father's special presence to mankind, the prophecies about the kingdom of God were to be fulfilled by him. For example, when he announced the beginning of his mission in his hometown of Nazareth, he got up at the synagogue service and read the passage from Isaiah that applied to him:

> The spirit of the Lord has been given to me,
> for he has anointed me.
> He has sent me to bring the good news to the poor,
> to proclaim liberty to captives
> and to the blind new sight,
> to set the downtrodden free,
> to proclaim the Lord's year of favour.
>
> (Lk 4:18-19)

In short, God's kingdom coming refers to the reality that the world is to be ruled by peace, justice and love. It means that in a special way God the Father is drawing all men, women and children to him. It means that in the person of his Son a certain activity has begun in the world that has an inevitable conclusion: the salvation of mankind and the union of the world with the Creator.

Jesus not only preached the fact of the reign of God, but he revealed himself and his kingdom in his signs (miracles) to demonstrate the power of God's presence and love. For example, he cured the demoniac to show that God's power is stronger than that of Satan (Lk 5:33-37). He tamed the raging storm to show that he has mastery over the forces of nature (Jn 6:16-21). He cured the blind man to indicate what power faith in him has (Jn 9:1-40). He raised the dead to life again, thus demonstrating that even death is conquered now that the Lord has come (Jn 11:1-44).

Connected with all of Jesus' teaching and miracles, though, was the call for men and women to turn from their lives of sin. Do you recall how Jesus rescued the adulteress from death? He turned away her accusers and gently forgave her. But he told her not to sin again (Jn 8:1-11). At times he used strong words to awaken his enemies. For example, he quoted Isaiah:

> This people honours me only with lip service while
> their hearts are far from me.
>
> (Mk 7:6)

At other times, he called them "blind guides, hypocrites, and whitewashed tombs" (see Mt 23:24-39).

Why did Jesus speak so forcefully? He simply felt an urgency that he was offering mankind the great gift of salvation and that his message was sometimes ignored by those who should have known better. There is a lesson in this for us today. Do we know better? Do we persist in living our lives as though our Lord has *not* come? Do we ignore the good news of God's kingdom? For example, do we continue to argue among ourselves, to complain about not owning the latest record album, to ignore the friendless, to live each day and never turn to God?

Conversion literally means turning our hearts away from our lives of sin, of complaining and fighting, of searching after the latest material things that we think will make us happy. Conversion means turning to our Lord Jesus, accepting him as our Savior and living our lives in accordance with his Father's will. It is a choice individuals could make 2,000 years ago. It is a choice that Jesus invites us to make today.

---

1. Read the following miracles of Jesus. Discuss how each illustrates the theme of conversion.

   a. Jn 2:1-11—water   b. Mt 15:21-28—
      into wine   Canaanite woman

   c. Lk 8:43-48—woman with hemorrhage

   d. Mk 10:46-52—blind Bartimaeus

2. Read the following two passages of Jesus about God's kingdom. What do they have in common; that is, what does Jesus claim will happen to the kingdom?

a. Mt 13:3-9; 18-23   b. Mk 4:26-29

3. One of the reasons we do not turn to the kingdom of God is that other things distract us from our true source of happiness. Advertisements for products bring home this point well. Ads sell not only products but also certain values behind the products. For example, an ad for a fancy car sells both the car and the value of prestige which is supposed to bring us happiness. Also, many cosmetics appeal to our desire to be attractive sexually to others—the key to happiness we are told.

Below are several descriptions for products. From ads and commercials find an example for each. Then list and discuss each value which is being sold along with the product. How might these values get in the way of God's kingdom?

General description	Example	Value Sold
a. Ad for liquor	_____	_____
b. Ad for soft drink	_____	_____
c. Ad for stereo equipment	_____	_____
d. Ad for perfume	_____	_____
e. Ad for a vacation in a resort area	_____	_____
f. Ad for breakfast food	_____	_____
g. Ad for detergent	_____	_____
h. Ad for clothing	_____	_____

III. God's Forgiveness. Jesus preached a strong message trying to get people to realize that God's kingdom is now working in their midst. He asks for nothing short of a total turning away from a life of sin, a conversion to faith in him and his Father. But the exciting part of his message is that his Father makes it possible for us to accept him and his kingdom because he forgives our sins, our failures, our shortcomings. He gently stands ready to touch our hearts if we are only open enough to receive the touch.

Jesus' message about his Father is one of incredible love. He often joined his power of healing the sick with his power to forgive sins. For example, when Jesus forgave the sins of the paralytic at Capernaum, he was accused by his enemies of claiming to do what only God could do. To back up his claim (and in effect give strong testimony to the fact that he was God), Jesus cured the man. Matthew notes the impact this miracle had on the crowd: They were awestruck (Mt 9:1-8). His love of sinners and his association with them made his enemies grumble and complain (Mt 11:19). Their lament was how could he—obviously a great teacher and a holy man—associate with such low-class people. Simon the Pharisee was especially perturbed when Jesus allowed a notorious woman sinner to anoint him at his (Simon's) dinner table (Lk 7:36-50).

A favorite teaching device of Jesus was the parable. He told many parables to demonstrate God's love of sinners and the forgiveness he extends to them. Luke 15 contains three famous examples of this kind of teaching. There, God the Father is compared to a woman who rejoices over finding a small coin; thus is God's joy when a sinner is found and returns to the Father. Again, he is compared to the good shepherd who seeks out the one lost sheep; such is God's concern for us sinners that he would leave the 99. Finally, we find in Lk 15:11-32 the story of the Prodigal Son who abandons his father, loses his inheritance, and ends up miserable. But the son remembers his father's love and returns home. Recall how the father runs out to embrace the son and celebrates his return. The father, who represents our loving God, does not dwell over the sin. He waited anxiously for his son to return and now joyfully loves his son. He doesn't seek vengeance. He has already forgotten the hurt. Such is God's love for us!

Jesus lived as well as preached forgiveness. Imagine the pain of Jesus hanging on the cross with men and women scorning him. Yet, what does he do? It is as if he wants to drive home the message of God's loving forgiveness with his last ounce of energy. First, he looks down from the cross at those who are mocking him and says, "Father, forgive them; they do not know what they are doing" (Lk 23:34). Second, he turns to a condemned criminal and tells him, "Indeed, I promise you, today you will be with me in paradise" (Lk 23:43).

The important lesson in all of this is that God's forgiveness is ours, too. It is there for the taking. When we fail to love others, when we lie, cheat, steal, fail in sexual morality, we are like the Prodigal Son who only had to turn to receive the gracious love and forgiveness of our loving Father.

As we shall see in this book, these themes of conversion and forgiveness recur whenever we meet our Lord sacramentally. Baptism is a new birth, a turning away from the life of sin, a new beginning. Confirmation extends this initial commitment to God's kingdom because we are given in a special way the strength of the Holy Spirit to live the challenge of the kingdom of God in our life. The sacrament of reconciliation is the gift of Jesus to his people to receive God's forgiveness. The sacrament of healing is another sign of our Lord's desire to strengthen us in those painful situations of sickness or near-death which might tempt us away from following his will. The Eucharist strengthens us daily in our resolve to live with Christ. Furthermore, the Eucharist helps reconcile us to the Father and to each other. It is a real participation in the sacrifice of Jesus' cross—a cross that lifts us from our sinfulness to a life with his Father in love.

IV. Jesus' Call to Unity. Did you ever notice how unity seems to be one of the great quests of human life? Note how ball players after a significant win credit their victory to the team spirit and the unity they shared. Some have even called their team a "family." Note, too, the lyrics of many songs. They often deal with "young love." The refrain to many of these songs is the desire for a oneness of mind, heart and body. Also, have you ever noticed how in times of national crisis a country will rally behind its leaders? The language used in times of national crisis often talks of "national unity."

One of the recurring themes in the teaching and life of our Lord is his stress on unity. John's Gospel especially highlights this theme. For example, John states with emphasis that Jesus died precisely to make us one (Jn 11:51). Furthermore, one of the most important prayers of Jesus was his prayer for believers that they might be united the way the Father and Jesus are united in perfect unity. In short, Jesus desires us to be one with him and the Father so that we may be one with each other (Jn 17:20-21).

We men and women desire unity with others more than almost anything else. This is certainly true of friends. Is it not true, though, that so often unity is an elusive thing that is very difficult to achieve?

The beauty of Jesus' message is that he can provide the unity we so desperately crave. As Jesus taught, he is the vine and we are the branches. His life flows through us and because this is so we are intimately related to each other. Another way of putting this same truth is that Jesus is the head of the body and we are its members (1 Cor 12:12). We are all related to the head (Jesus) and thus related to each other.

Jesus saw better than anyone that we are all children of God, his Father. He knew better than anyone that he is brother to us all. Because this is true, we are related to him as brother or sister. In a certain sense, we are related to each other even more intimately than blood brothers and sisters.

When the apostles came to Jesus and asked him how they should pray, he taught them the great prayer, the Our Father. He invited us to call God "Father" (Mt 6:9-15). There are two very important insights that are associated with calling God "Father." For one thing, the term Jesus used in his native language to address God was *Abba*. He invites us to use this same term! *Abba* literally is translated "dada, daddy." "Dada" carries with it the kind of intimacy, trust, love and gentleness a very young child has for its father. For us to call our God *Abba* means that we are very special people who know firsthand that God loves us with the openness and gentleness that good human fathers have for their own children. How special we are as God's creatures to have such a warm relationship with him!

Second, to call God *Abba* means that we are members of a spiritual family, a family united in the oneness of Jesus Christ. What "good news" this is! To realize that the oneness we strive for has been achieved for us by our brother Jesus should help us look at each other in a new light. It might also help us relate to each other with much more love and compassion.

This theme of unity is very important when studying the sacraments. Baptism unites us to Christ as it initiates us into his Body, the people of God. Confirmation gives us in a deeper way the Holy Spirit who St. Paul repeatedly teaches is the principle of unity, the Spirit who enables us to call God *Abba* (Gal 4:6). The Eucharist is the food of unity. By receiving Christ's body and blood we are united to our Lord and more deeply to each other. The sacrament of reconciliation helps reunify us with the community which we may have harmed through our sinfulness. The sacrament of the sick strengthens our bond of unity with the Lord in the difficult time of illness or near-death. The sacraments of vocation—marriage and ordination—stress the unity of the married couple with the Lord and the priest-minister with the Christian community.

REFLECTION AND DISCUSSION

A. What meaning do the following terms hold for you?

    1. dada: _____

    2. daddy: _____

    3. dad: _____

    4. pop: _____

    5. father: _____

    6. "old man": _____

B. Read and meditate on the Our Father, Mt. 6:9-15 or Lk 11:2-4.

In a real way, the Our Father unites the themes of forgiveness and oneness. Our *Abba* expects us to forgive the faults of others because he has forgiven us. Further, he expects us to forgive because we are his children, brothers and sisters to each other and to our Lord Jesus.

And yet forgiveness is one of the hardest things to show to others. Why not take stock of your "forgiveness quotient" by examining yourself on how you forgive others who have harmed you? Mark the following "sins" according to the scale below.

1—this is easy for me to forgive

2—I have some difficulty forgiving this

3—this is very difficult to forgive

____ someone talks behind my back

____ someone lies to me

____ someone cheats me

____ someone steals from me

____ someone swears at me or cusses me out

____ someone spreads rumors about me

____ someone physically harms me

____ someone I counted on lets me down

QUESTIONS:

1. How would your answers change if the "someone" were a good friend?

2. How do you verbally forgive someone? How do you nonverbally show forgiveness? (Is saying "I forgive you" different from saying "It's OK"? By the same token, is there a difference between "I apologize" and "I ask for your forgiveness"?)

3. Discuss these three quotes. Do you agree with them?

a. "It is easier for the generous to forgive, than for the offender to ask forgiveness."—James Thomson, poet

b. " 'I can forgive, but I cannot forget' is only another way of saying, 'I will not forgive.'—Forgiveness ought to be like a cancelled note—torn in two, and burned up, so that it never can be shown against one."—H. W. Beecher, 19th-century American clergyman

c. [You must forgive] "not seven times; but seventy times seven times."—Jesus to Peter, Mt 18:22

V. The Message of Love. The word *love* sums up the message and the life of Jesus of Nazareth. What a simple statement to make. There is a problem, though, in the assertion that Jesus represents love. The problem rests in the many ways we use the word *love* in the English language. For example, I can say that I love pizza or that I love to play golf. I might also say I'm going to "make love" with my wife. Finally, I can say I love my little girl. In all these cases, love is used in different ways. In one case, it involves my "liking" a thing (pizza); in another, it means liking to do a certain activity. In a third case, it refers to sexual expression while in the fourth situation it refers to my attitude and way of relating to another person.

In short, *love* is a word that can be used in many different contexts. Some people even cheapen the word by using it to refer to promiscuous sex as in the term "free love." Still others think they are clever by repeating a cliche that makes the fuzzy distinction, "I have to love you but I don't have to like you."

Because the word *love* is used in so many ways, people have a difficult time knowing precisely what is meant by saying the message and life of Jesus are characterized by love. Does this mean Jesus was sentimental? Does it mean he was a pushover and that he wants his followers to be pushovers? Does it mean that he went through life with blinders on, ignoring the evil that is present in human life?

For Jesus, love is a manly/womanly word. It means reverence and responsibility, loyalty and knowledge. It means acceptance of one for what one is. For Jesus, love means service. Jesus' message first and foremost is that his Father loves us. The Father created us from nothing and gives us life. The Father gives us his greatest gift, his Son Jesus. In return, the Father wants our love. Our love is expressed by keeping the commandments (1 Jn 5:3) and by being like the one we greatly admire—Jesus (Jn 15:9).

One of the most powerful and exciting truths Jesus taught us is that love of God and love of neighbor are *one*. The love of God and of our neighbor is *active*. What we do or fail to do for the hungry, the thirsty, the homeless, the naked, the sick, the imprisoned, the least of these, we do or fail to do for our Lord (Mt 25:31-46). The true test of love is whether we can love even our enemies. This is the theme of the parable of the Good Samaritan (Lk 10:29-37) who *actively* went out of his way to love his enemy.

There is nothing sentimental or weak about Jesus' concept of love. He calls on us, his followers, to imitate him. He asks us to serve others by washing feet. By this he means that we should be willing to humble ourselves; to help others as he did at the Last Supper (Jn 13:1-17). We are called to love others as Jesus has loved us. Often little gratitude is shown in return for our love. Sometimes even hostility is given in return. Loving is difficult and demanding work, but work that Christians are called to do. This is how we are to be known as his followers: that we love each other (Jn 13:34-35).

Jesus loved even to death on the cross. The ultimate sign of love is that we be willing to give up our lives for others the way our Lord did. "The greatest love a person can have for his friends is to give his life for them" (Jn 15:13). Most of us will never be called on to give up our physical lives for another. But all of us are called on daily to die a little bit to our own self-centeredness. We "die to ourselves" when we forgive others, when we respect and care for others. This kind of love takes courage and strength. It demands faith and trust in God. It is the heart of our religion and the good news we are privileged to live daily in our life of response to God and his children, our sisters and brothers.

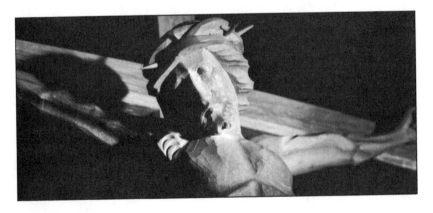

THE MESSAGE OF LOVE

1. Jesus said that we will live in his love if we keep his commandments (Jn 15:10). In a real way, the Beatitudes are Jesus' commandments for his followers. Read the Beatitudes, Mt 5:3-12. Give an example from your own life of how you have lived or can live each of the Beatitudes. Briefly explain how your example is really a form of love.

Beatitude	Example	How this is love
1. Blest are the poor in spirit.		
2. Blest are the sorrowing.		
3. Blest are the lowly.		
4. Blest are they who hunger and thirst for holiness.		
5. Blest are they who show mercy.		
6. Blest are the single-hearted.		
7. Blest are the peacemakers.		
8. Blest are those persecuted for holiness' sake.		
9. Blest are you when they insult you . . . because of me.		

2. Pick out three of your favorite songs that deal in some way or another with the theme of love. Bring the words to class and explain how the lyrics either agree or disagree with

Jesus' concept of love. What kind of love do they set forth as ideal? How would they stand up to Jesus' ideas on love?

3. Read and meditate on the following scriptural passages on love:

   a. 1 Cor 13: the qualities of love

   b. Jn 15: Jesus' discourse on love

   c. Mt 25:31-46: the union of love of God and love of others.

      Do you know anyone who loves like this? If so, share with your classmates.

4. Interview the following people and get their definition of love:

   a. A small child (perhaps a small brother or sister)

   b. Your parents

   c. A college student

   d. A young married couple

   e. A priest or deacon

   f. A friend

5. Write your own definition of love:_____

   _____

   _____

   _____

   _____

VI. Jesus as the Message. This chapter has tried to point out the good news of Jesus. Jesus taught that God's kingdom has come and that this reality demands conversion on our part. He taught that forgiveness, unity and love are at the heart of the kingdom. But an extremely important part of his message includes Jesus himself. This fantastic truth is highlighted by St. John in his Gospel. There Jesus says, "I am the Way, the Truth, and the Life; no one can come to the Father except through me" (Jn 14:6).

Jesus is the way, the truth and the life. To believe this statement is to find meaning and happiness in life. Jesus is the *way* in that he is the one who takes us to the Father. He is our Savior (the name *Jesus* means "savior") who overcomes sin and death, the two barriers to union with God. Jesus is the *truth* in that he is "where it is at." God the Father lives in him and speaks through him (Jn 14:10). What Jesus teaches and does corresponds to what is really real, it is in union with the one we call God. To hear him is to hear the truth. Jesus is *life* because through his suffering, death and resurrection, sin and death (the ultimate effect of sin) are conquered. If we join ourselves to the Risen Lord, we too will share in his triumph over death.

The sacraments celebrate Jesus as the way, the truth and the life. They celebrate the Paschal Mystery. The Paschal Mystery is the truth of our faith that Jesus suffered, died, rose from the dead and is glorified with the Father. Jesus allowed evil and sin to destroy him so that his Father could raise him and glorify him to show that evil and death are conquered through him. In Jesus, death does not have the last word. Life does. Jesus' resurrection and glorification assure us that our destiny is not an eternity of nothingness in a grave. Rather, his resurrection and glorification have won for us superabundant life with him and his Father in union with the Holy Spirit.

What remains for us is to meet this Jesus who has conquered death. What remains for us is to accept this Jesus as our Savior and our Lord. We do this when we realize in faith that Jesus lives in the world today and that we can contact him. It follows, then, that if you want true meaning in life, then *meet Jesus Christ*. If you want the truth, meet your friend and brother, Jesus. If you want to live life to its fullest, allow Jesus Christ to touch you.

This book is about one of the key ways Christians believe they can come into contact with the Lord in the world today. It is about the sacraments, those signs that put us into touch with our Lord. Read on to see how this is done and to see how you might draw closer to our Lord.

FINDING JESUS

Christians through the ages have especially felt close to God/
Jesus in some of the following circumstances. Check those
which have been meaningful encounters for you.

_____ in an intimate con-
versation with a close
friend

_____ looking at a sunset

_____ praying alone in a
candlelit room

_____ after receiving Holy
Communion

_____ watching children
play

_____ listening to some
beautiful music

_____ walking alone in the
woods

_____ meditating alone in a
quiet church

_____ praying and worshipping with others

_____ observing the joy on
a person's face who
benefited from your
kindness

_____ reading the Bible

_____ seeing a newborn
infant

_____ witnessing to Christ
at a youth retreat

_____ receiving/giving forgiveness

_____ observing an elderly
person in prayer

Add a few of your own encounters here and share them with a
classmate.

a. _____   b. _____

c. _____

Discuss the following passages. How might each be considered
a way of meeting the Lord?

"For where two or three meet in my name, I shall
be there with them" (Mt 18:20).

"I tell you solemnly, in so far as you did this for
one of the least of these brothers of mine, you did
it for me" (Mt 25:40).

SUMMARY

The following statements capture the major points made in this first chapter. They may be of help as you review the themes discussed.

1. In searching for meaning in life, people should seriously consider the help Jesus Christ might give in the search.

2. "The Incarnation" refers to the belief that in Jesus God became man. The "incarnational principle" refers to the reality that human life and all connected with it are worthy because God became one of us.

3. Jesus' message can be summarized as follows: God's kingdom has come. Therefore, turn from your life of sin and accept Jesus. The great sign of the kingdom is the Father's loving forgiveness. In unity with the Spirit, Jesus himself calls us into unity with his Father, himself and every other human. Thus, we should imitate Jesus. We imitate Jesus by loving. Love is the command Jesus gave to his followers and what he demonstrated in a supreme way on the cross.

4. Jesus is his message. The Paschal Mystery of his suffering, death, resurrection and glorification has won for us eternal life.

5. The sacraments are signs of encounter with Jesus today. They celebrate the Paschal Mystery, the coming of God's kingdom, forgiveness, unity and love.

EVALUATION

At the end of each chapter there will be a short quiz or essay question to test your understanding of the material of the chapter. You may wish to write these essays in a journal which you will keep until the end of the course.

Essay: In a few pages state in your own words what the message of
Jesus is. Then, briefly comment on what this message
means to you.

ADDITIONAL EXERCISES

1. Service Project

Jesus' message of love demands that we respond to "the least
of these." As a class, make up a list of people in the neighborhood
of your school who need help. You may list old people, handicapped children, poor people, the sick, etc. Then devise a project
of service that will last for the duration of the course. Some ideas:

   a. Raise money through bake sales.

   b. Hold a canned food drive.

   c. Establish a program of visitation for the elderly.

   d. Take magazines and newspapers to shut-ins.

   e. Volunteer to do odd jobs for the sick and/or old; for ex-
       ample, yard work, snow shoveling, shopping, etc.

   f. Put on a seasonal party for handicapped or retarded chil-
       dren in the neighborhood.

   g. Volunteer your services to a parish group that does any of
       the above.

2. Witness Project

Find one person who is willing to listen and share what you
learned in this chapter. Ask the person what he or she thinks of
"Jesus' message."

3. Creative Project

Select one of the themes discussed in the chapter, for example, the role of the Incarnation. Put together a slide show with
music illustrating the theme. Your class might want to use the

presentation for a eucharistic celebration or a penance service later in the course.

4. Bible Project

Do one of the following:

a. In one sitting, read Mark's Gospel. Write a reflection on who is Jesus in this particular Gospel.

b. Read one of St. Paul's letters. A good choice would be his First Letter to the Corinthians. What does St. Paul believe about Jesus?

2

What Is a Sacrament?

. . . Christ is always present in his church, especially in her liturgical celebrations. He is present in the sacrifice of the Mass, not only in the person of his minister, . . . but especially under the Eucharistic species. By his power he is present in the sacraments, so that when a man baptizes it is really Christ himself who baptizes. He is present in his Word, since it is he himself who speaks when the Holy Scriptures are read in the church. He is present, finally, when the church prays and sings, for he promised: "Where two or three are gathered together for my sake, there am I in the midst of them" (Mt 18:20).
—Vatican Council II, Constitution on the Sacred Liturgy, #7

Before we take up a discussion of the individual sacraments and how they help us meet the Risen Lord, this chapter will present several definitions of *sacrament*. We will begin by looking at the foundations of sacramental reality. Then, we will discuss several classic definitions of sacrament, there treating the role of Jesus, the church and the individual Christian. The chapter will conclude with some remarks about the seven sacraments in particular and about grace, a traditional concept in Catholic theology and belief.

Let's begin our discussion with the following exercise which deals with symbols, a concept which is basic to the sacraments.

35

Part 1: Word Association. Below are listed a number of words that describe different realities. Please jot down the first thing that comes to mind when you see the word.

sunset: _____

kiss: _____

turkey: _____

hammer and sickle: _____

red rose: _____

smile: _____

American flag: _____

Part 2: Personal Symbols. Each person is unique. We often attach special meaning to things that either display our uniqueness or represent our deepest feelings and desires. Below is a "personality grid." Please draw some symbol (or write a word) for each item listed in the circles below. The symbol should reflect your uniqueness.

1. your most prized possession
2. your greatest personal achievement to date
3. what you would most like to be
4. the person you most admire
5. something that best describes your personality

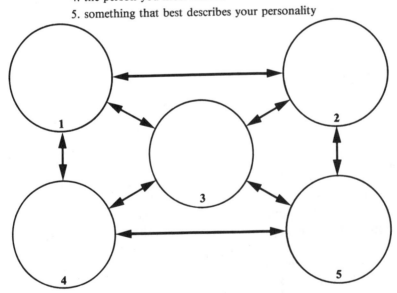

Part 3: Discussion

1. Share responses to Part 1 with your classmates. Were their choices similar to yours? Why or why not? Do some things convey the same meaning to most people? Would a blind person answer these differently? Explain.

2. Have someone in class who knows you fairly well try to guess the meaning of your "personality grid." Why did you choose the particular symbols/signs that you did? Is it important for people to use symbols? Why or why not?

FOUNDATIONS OF SACRAMENTAL REALITY

To understand the meaning of the term *sacrament,* it is first necessary to reflect on two observations that seem pretty true about human life. These observations can help us appreciate and reflect on the nature of sacramental reality.

● **Observation #1:** Things, events and persons tend to point to a meaning beyond themselves.
● **Observation #2:** The human mind has a capacity for making symbols.

These observations really go hand in hand. What they are saying is that reality is basically symbolic and that people are able to perceive, understand and make symbols.

For example, when you see someone smile, you know the person is probably happy or amused. The person does not have to tell you what he or she is feeling because you know that a smile is a sign of happiness or amusement. The symbol—a smile—points to the reality of happiness/amusement.

For our purposes, a symbol can be defined as *something concrete that represents something else.* It is a sign that points to another reality.

Signs and symbols are all around us. Observation #1 says that things, events and people have the capacity to be symbols. For example, consider the following *things.* An American flag is a special piece of cloth, colored and shaped a certain way. For Americans, it represents freedom and democracy. For enemies of America, it may represent something negative like imperialism. Another symbolic thing is a stop sign. It is an octagonal shape that communicates to a driver of a car that he or she had better brake the car or risk hurting someone or risk getting a traffic ticket. Consider a few more examples. The color blue is found in many things and communicates moods like peacefulness, coolness, calmness. A kiss usually represents love and friendship. Fire can mean warmth and coziness; it can also mean destruction and death. A particular perfume or after-shave cologne may remind you of a certain person you like—or dislike. We can go on and on because almost every *thing* has the capacity of being a symbol, a sign pointing to some other reality.

What about *events?* What do the following mean to you? July 4? December 25? February 14? The last Thursday of November? On the first date we commemorate the signing of the Declaration of Independence, the date traditionally celebrated as the birth of the United States. On the second date, we celebrate the birth of Jesus. It usually brings to mind feelings of family fellowship and love. It is a special day with much meaning for Christians. February 14 is Valentine's Day. It means candy. It also means rejoicing in friendship with a loved one. In the United States, the last Thursday of November is Thanksgiving Day, a special day on which Americans thank God for the blessings given to them. It also means family and good things to eat. As a final example, consider the most special day in the year: your birthday. To most people, your birthday is just another day. To you it is special because it marks your advent into the world; it notes your uniqueness.

And *persons*—how can they be symbols? Think of John Fitzgerald Kennedy, Mother Teresa of Calcutta, Pope John Paul II, Joe DiMaggio and Abraham Lincoln. All of these people are symbols who have special meaning for some people. JFK represents for your parents and many of their generation a period of their youth, a period of hope and idealism in American political life. Mother Teresa is a living sign of God's love for the poor. For the whole world, Pope John Paul II represents Roman Catholicism.

He not only heads the church, for many people he *is* the church. He is their only link to Catholicism. Joe DiMaggio has been immortalized in song. He somehow represents the "good old days" of baseball when baseball was more of an innocent game than the big business it has become today. Incidentally, he has also become *the* symbol of a certain product. To see Joe DiMaggio is to think of the product. Finally, Abraham Lincoln has become the sign of equality, the realization of the American dream. His leadership during the time of the American Civil War has won for him a privileged place in history. Many leaders look to his example and his strength today as they try to make important decisions.

Things, events and people all have the capacity to make present a reality greater than ourselves. They can be and often are symbols of something other than themselves. This is true because men and women are capable of making, recognizing and understanding symbols. The very letters you are reading are signs that point to ideas. Speech and words are perhaps our most important symbols because they enable us to communicate, to share the invisible world of ideas.

What can we conclude from these two observations? Simply put, reality is symbolic. Humans use symbols to convey meaning, to get at what is real. Humans make symbols to communicate about themselves and what they think is important. In short, humans and their world are symbolic.

PLUNGING DEEPER: MORE ON SYMBOLS

Another way of looking at symbols is by type. One classification of symbols notes three kinds: conventional symbols, accidental symbols and universal symbols.

1. A *conventional symbol* is something that people in a particular society agree means one thing and not another. An example is the word *table*. The letters t-a-b-l-e mean one thing in countries where English is spoken. But in countries where Spanish is spoken the letters m-e-s-a are used to convey the same meaning as t-a-b-l-e. Language is a convention (a customary way of communicating) that people within a given area use to convey meaning.

Another example is a flag. People attach special meaning that can vary from flag to flag. Custom both makes the symbol and determines its meaning.

2. An *accidental symbol* is something that has special meaning for you as an individual, but may have very little meaning for someone else. Think of two lovers. When they fell in love, perhaps a certain song was popular. In the future, when they hear the song, all kinds of pleasant, warm memories come to mind. When you hear the song, it may do nothing for you. Certain smells may be accidental symbols, too. For example, when you smell a certain perfume, does it remind you of someone? When you smell a particular odor in the air, does it bring back memories of a special time in your life? The possibilities for accidental symbols are limitless.

3. A *universal symbol* is something that means pretty much the same thing to all men and women at all times in all places. Fire is a good example. Everyone interprets fire as the source of life and light. In addition, fire means destruction and death. Another popular universal symbol is water. Water means renewal, rebirth, life. But like fire it can also mean death and destruction. The church has effectively used universal symbols in its celebration of the seven sacraments. These speak a common meaning to men and women in all countries. Water, fire, incense, bread and wine are a few of these universal symbols.

EXERCISES:

1. Find three insignia or logos from advertisements that are immediately recognized as *conventional* symbols. For example, "golden arches" are interpreted as a sign of a particular brand of food. Bring these insignia or logos into class and share them with your classmates.

   Discuss: Can you identify any factors that are involved in the making of conventional symbols?

2. List three *accidental* symbols that convey special meaning for you. Explain what each one means for you and why it got that meaning.

Symbol	What it means	Source of meaning
a. _____	_____	_____
b. _____	_____	_____
c. _____	_____	_____

3. Colors usually have a symbolic meaning. Research the meaning of the following colors.

Color	Meaning(s)
a. White	_____
b. Red	_____
c. Black	_____
d. Green	_____
e. Purple	_____

   As a class, list ways the church uses various colors in its liturgical celebrations.

SACRAMENTAL REALITY

Let's begin our consideration of the concept of sacrament by looking at three definitions of sacrament. After discussing each of these briefly, we will turn to Jesus, the church and the Christian as participants in the "sacramental reality."

Definition 1: St. Paul provides us our first definition of sacrament. In the Latin bible, the word "sacramentum" is used to translate the Greek word *mysterion* (mystery). "Mystery" is the term St. Paul used when he referred to God's hidden plan of always wanting to save, renew and unite all things in Christ (Eph 1:9; 3:3, 9 NAB). God's mystery, his sacrament according to St. Paul, is revealed most perfectly in our Savior Jesus, the person who unifies us and reconciles us with the Father.

Definition 2: St. Augustine's definition of sacrament stressed the notion of sign or symbol. For Augustine, a sacrament was *a sign of a sacred reality.* It is a holy sign—a symbol or image or expression—through which the believer can both *perceive* and *receive* an invisible grace. The sign or symbol points to the deeper reality of the spiritual world, a world where friendship with God can be realized. Thus, for example, the waters of baptism point to the rebirth of a Christian in friendship with our Lord. The waters (a thing) help the Christian perceive the reality of rebirth; but because baptism is a *sacrament,* the grace of rebirth is truly *received.*

Definition 3: St. Thomas Aquinas provided quite a bit of precision in his definition of a sacrament. For him, a sacrament was an *efficacious symbol.* What is meant by that? Well, an "efficacious symbol" is one that effects what it symbolizes and symbolizes what it effects. What is symbolized happens. An ordinary symbol or sign points to a deeper reality; it doesn't cause it. Thus, for example, a stop sign indicates that the driver should brake the car. But the stop sign—because it is an ordinary symbol/sign—does not *cause* the person to stop. It merely points to the reality, to the notion of stopping. A sacrament, though, is a special sign that brings about what it symbolizes and symbolizes what it brings about. For example, the bread and wine in the celebration of the Mass are symbols that point to the body and blood of Jesus. But because the Eucharist is a sacrament (more than just an ordinary symbol), the bread and wine *become* (are) the body and blood of Christ, though still remaining *visible* signs. In a very special way, the sacrament is a sign that we can perceive through our senses which puts us into real contact with the saving Jesus. In a sacrament, there is a *pointing to* and an *effecting of* the reality symbolized. Thus, a sacrament is a very special kind of symbol.

JESUS CHRIST: THE FIRST SACRAMENT

The three definitions of sacrament given above are very traditional. Most of us have come to talk of sacrament in terms of the seven sacraments which are part of the liturgical life of the church. But the Second Vatican Council has helped us broaden our understanding of the term *sacrament* to include Jesus, the church and the individual Christian.

How might Jesus Christ fit our definition of sacrament? In a number of ways. First, he is the mystery (definition #1) of God's love for mankind. In him, the mystery comes close to us. In him, God's plan of salvation and reconciliation has taken place. He was the perfect "man for others" who gave up his life so that we might live. In Jesus, God's loving kindness reaches its fullest expression.

Second, this loving kindness made visible in Jesus is the great sign of God in our midst (Emmanuel—God with us). Jesus is the sign (definition #2), the symbol of God's total love for us. To understand what Jesus stands for is to understand how God loves us. As we saw in Chapter 1, Jesus' message, his life and his person are signs that point to the really real, to the Father and his plan of incredible love for mankind. Reflect on Jesus' words once again: "I am the Way, the Truth, and the Life; and no one can come to the Father except through me" (Jn 14:6). Jesus is the great sign—God made flesh, God made visible—who points us to our destiny and helps us achieve that destiny. In this way, Jesus is the great sacrament, the prime or first sacrament. In him, God became visible—available to us.

Third, Jesus is an "efficacious sign" (definition #3). His passion, death, resurrection and glorification point to the reality that sin and death have been conquered, that eternal life with the Father is a reality. Because Jesus is a sacrament, he not only points to these realities, he makes them possible for us to achieve today.

For the cured leper, Jesus' touch was a sacrament, a visible sign of God's loving action. Jesus' kind glances and reassuring touches and life-giving words are signs of the Father's love and concern. This same Jesus is present today in the seven sacraments. He comes to us in the visible signs of words, wine and bread, water and oil. He comes to cure us and to take us to his loving Father. This Word-made-flesh, this visible symbol of God's love, is working in the world today. As Pope Leo the Great expressed it: "Whatever was visible in our Redeemer has passed over into the sacraments." We need but turn in faith to our Lord who is visible to us under the signs of the sacraments and allow him to touch us today.

EXERCISES:

Part 1: The New Testament relates a number of stories about people who reluctantly approached Jesus or who had difficulty approaching him, the sacrament of God's love. Listed below are several of these people. Research the bible references for each of these people and jot down the reason for their difficulty or reluctance. Then, list what happened after they mustered up the courage to meet Jesus.

Person(s)	*Reason for reluctance*	*What happened?*
1. Woman with hemorrhage (Lk 8:42-48)		
2. Woman at well (Jn 4:5-42)		
3. Nicodemus (Jn 3:1-21)		
4. Paralytic at Capernaum (Mk 2:1-12)		
5. Peter (Lk 22:54-62)		
6. The disciples (Lk 24:9-12)		
7. Sick man at Bethesda (Jn 5:1-9)		

Part 2: At times you may have reluctantly approached Jesus or felt that you were unable to approach him. Which of the

reasons below may have kept you from meeting Jesus in prayer
or through the sacraments?

_____ laziness

_____ afraid of what
others might think

_____ wasn't sure he was
there

_____ a feeling of un-
worthiness

_____ couldn't find the
time

_____ don't really be-
lieve that Jesus is
still with us

_____ hard to see him
sometimes, espe-
cially at Mass

_____ Other reason(s):__

_____ could not see that
I need him

Please discuss:

1. Which of the above were merely excuses? Were any of them
   valid reasons?

2. Were you like any of the persons in the first part of the
   exercise? Explain.

3. Based on what you have read in these first two chapters
   plus your own experiences, what might you tell someone
   who is afraid to meet Jesus?

The CHURCH: Sacrament of Jesus

The Spirit of Jesus, the Holy Spirit, was given to the church on Pentecost Sunday. (Read Acts 2:1-12.) The Spirit, who is the gift of God's presence in the Christian community, is the great gift of the love between the Father and the Son superbly demonstrated by Jesus dying so that we may live and the Father raising Christ up so that eternal life can be ours.

The presence of Jesus in the church, in the Christian community, makes the church a kind of sacrament. The Vatican II document entitled *The Dogmatic Constitution on the Church* says it well:

> By her relationship with Christ, the Church is a kind of sacrament of intimate union with God, and of the unity of all mankind, that is, she is a sign and an instrument of such union and unity. (#1)

Who Is the Church? The church is the Body of Christ. This body is made up of the head (Jesus) and the members, each individual who comes together to worship the Father in unity with Jesus and the Holy Spirit. The church is the people of God.

By calling the church "a kind of sacrament," Vatican II is stressing that the life of the members of the church is a *sign* that points to the intimate union between God and us which Jesus has achieved. Furthermore, the church is an *instrument,* that is, a means or a way by which we can be unified.

What does this mean? To the degree that the church worships the Father faithfully and witnesses to Jesus lovingly, to that degree the church makes Jesus and his love visible for men and women to see. To the degree that the church is true to her founder, to that degree she helps bring about the union Jesus prayed for in John's Gospel.

What a tremendous privilege this is for you! As a Christian who loves and witnesses to Jesus, you are able to show others the true meaning of life: that God became man; that God forgives and loves us; that sin and death are conquered; that we are destined for an eternal life of happiness with our creator. In a real way, you are a kind of sacrament. Because Jesus is present to you, you can bring him into the world today. You are Jesus' hands and feet, his smile and his comforting touch, his kind words and warm embrace. If you go out of your way to help others, if you are patient, if you forgive, if you love—if you do these things in our Lord's name—you become a concrete sign that points to our Lord, the life he lived, the message he delivered, the victory he has won. If you are a believable sign, if the church is a credible witness to the source of her life, you as a member of the church help draw men, women and children together on their journey to the Father.

But people sometimes fail to see Jesus in the world today because we Christians sin. We fail to be sacraments of Jesus, to live his love. When we are jealous or greedy or non-forgiving we obscure the good news of salvation. Instead of letting light shine before others, we hide our light under the basket of sin. Our task is simple, yet difficult. It is simple in that we have our Lord's strength and Spirit to guide us as we lead others to the Father. It is difficult because we so often lack the faith and resolve to live as faithful, loving members of Christ's body. To be "a kind of sacrament" means to be a sign that others can see, respect and admire. This is the task of the church and each individual in it. This is your task.

FOR FURTHER REFLECTION

1. Discuss how the church fits the various definitions of sacrament found below. Give concrete examples.

   a. *mystery* of God's salvation:

   b. *sign* of a sacred reality:

   c. *efficacious sign:*

2. One way for the Christian to be a sign is to follow Jesus' teaching: "You are the salt of the earth. . . . You are the light of the world. . . . Your light must shine before men so that they may see goodness in your acts and give praise to your heavenly Father (Mt 5:13,14,16 NAB). Rank in order of importance to you the following good deeds of a "sacrament" of Jesus.

    _____ A. Goes to Mass every Sunday
    _____ B. Is loyal to members of his or her family
    _____ C. Spends time helping old people
    _____ D. Avoids bad language
    _____ E. Prays often
    _____ F. Is honest all the time
    _____ G. Works in the pro-life movement
    _____ H. Helps fellow students at their studies
    _____ I. Tries to live a simple life

Discuss:
  a. Why did you choose as you did?
  b. Is one action more "believable" to you than another?
  c. Which of these would most impress a fellow Christian?
     a non-believer?

3. *Witness Situations:* To follow Jesus and be a credible
witness to him and his message takes hard, sometime courageous work. Below are several situations. Briefly say
what you would ordinarily do in that situation. Then check
off any of your responses that would make you proud of
yourself.

Situation	*What you normally would do*	*(✓)*
a. You read about some poor people in the neighbor- hood of your school who have been left homeless be- cause of a fire	_____ _____ _____ _____	____
b. You witness a youth shoplift in a record store	_____ _____ _____	____
c. You see a lonely student eat lunch by herself at school each day	_____ _____ _____ _____	____
d. You hear that the Senate is debating a bill to limit immi- gration from Southeast Asia	_____ _____ _____ _____	____
e. A friend makes some blasphemous comments about Jesus in your presence	_____ _____ _____	____

STILL ANOTHER VIEW OF *SACRAMENT*

The previous section gave some traditional theological definitions of *sacrament*. One can define sacrament in a very general way, too. In its broadest sense, a sacrament can be any person, event or thing through which we contact, encounter or experience God in a new or deeper way. With this definition in mind, it is rather easy to see how many other religious traditions have special symbols that are "sacramental" for them. These events, persons or things—which are part of their religious tradition—help them contact, encounter or experience God as he makes himself known to them.

Do a bit of research. Find out some of the special, meaningful symbols found in the following religions. List a particular symbol and discuss how it is meant to put the believer in that religious tradition into deeper contact with God.

Religion	Meaningful Symbols	Interpretation
1. Islam	_____	_____
2. A native American religion	_____	_____
3. Judaism	_____	_____
4. Buddhism	_____	_____
5. Ancient Greek or Roman religion	_____	_____

Name some experiences in your life in which you have "encountered God" in a special way.

a. _____

b. _____

c. _____

THE SEVEN SACRAMENTS

Most Catholics think of the seven *ritual* sacraments when they hear the word "sacrament." From this point on in the book, we will generally be discussing the seven sacraments. But it is important to realize that the seven sacraments flow from Jesus who is the first sacrament of our encounter with God and from the church which is the sacrament of Jesus. The seven sacraments belong to the church as high points of meeting the risen Jesus.

Most of your parents learned the following definition of a sacrament when they were young: *A sacrament is an outward sign instituted by Christ to give grace.* This definition still has merit, but it needs some explanation.

1. *A sacrament is a sign.* As we have already seen, a sacrament is a special visible (outward) sign that puts us into contact with our Lord. The seven ritual sacraments, furthermore, are particular signs that represent particular actions and values of Jesus. These signs re-enact and re-present what has taken place in the past. They make present and real today what Jesus has accomplished by his saving deeds. For example, the Eucharist is a symbolic (that is, sacramental and real) re-enactment of the Last Supper. Through immersion in water baptism represents conversion and death to sin. The seven signs also reflect Jesus' basic values; for example, forgiveness (sacrament of reconciliation), unity of the community (Eucharist), and healing (sacrament of anointing of the sick).

2. *A sacrament was instituted by Christ.* The sacraments are ultimately traceable to Jesus. His presence in the church through the Holy Spirit has helped the Christian community to discover those key moments in the life of the community and in the life of the individual when special help, grace and friendship with God are needed. In his own ministry, Jesus often came to people at the time of their greatest need: when people were sick, when they needed forgiveness, when they were beginning married life. The seven sacraments highlight the Paschal Mystery, the message of Jesus, the meaning of Jesus. They help us remember what Jesus Christ has done for us, and they enable us to celebrate his glorious deeds today. They are real points of encounter with Jesus.

3. *A sacrament gives grace.* One danger in using the term *grace* is to think of it as some thing, rather than a living relationship with God. Very simply, Jesus is grace. Grace is the *gift* of God's friendship for us. Grace is the story of God's constant love for us. Grace is God's free invitation to us to live in union with him.

What happens when we meet our Lord in one of the seven sacraments? For one thing, we meet God. In a sense, a sacrament is a promised meeting of Jesus and through him the Father. Our Lord promised that he would be with us; the seven sacraments are guaranteed moments of encountering him. They are grace-filled moments.

Because we encounter Jesus and the Father in the seven sacraments, we can change. The decision, though, is ours. If we *faith*fully accept God's friendship in the particular sacrament, we grow in friendship, our relationship deepens. We grow in grace. We get closer to Jesus. We live a life more deeply in union with our friend and our Father. What is needed on our part is a response to God's free offer. It takes faith. It takes saying "yes" to the gift (grace) offered.

Saying "yes" to Jesus in the sacraments results in the gift of the Holy Spirit living in us. The Spirit helps us to decide for Jesus and what he stands for. The Spirit enables us to live as members of God's kingdom and family. The gift of the Spirit also produces gifts in us—gifts like love, joy, peace, patient endurance, kindness, generosity, faith, mildness and chastity (Gal 5:22 NAB).

GIFTS OF THE HOLY SPIRIT AND YOU

Think of an example for both home and school where you could or did live each of the following gifts of the Spirit.

Gift	Home	School
joy	_____	_____
peace	_____	_____
patience	_____	_____
mildness	_____	_____

What does a sacrament do? The three functions of a sacrament are discussed below.

1. The seven sacraments *commemorate what happened in the*

past. They *celebrate the Paschal Mystery.* Each sacrament recalls the saving deeds of Jesus. In this way sacraments keep us in touch with our Christian heritage. They re-enact in symbol the actions and values of Jesus. They recapture his message of conversion, forgiveness, love and unity. They remind us that Jesus made all of life holy—from womb to tomb—birth and growth, meals and marriage, vocation and sickness. They serve to remind us that the source of our life and union with God the Father is Jesus. He is the important message the sacraments continually point to.

2. The seven sacraments *demonstrate in the present that Jesus Christ lives.* The sacraments bring about an actual meeting with Jesus through signs. His saving life and power which proceed from his death, resurrection and glorification are made available to us when we receive the sacraments.

3. The seven sacraments *prefigure our glorious future with Christ at the end of time.* Our ultimate goal in life is union with the Father in heaven. The sacraments point to this day in the future and because of the power of Jesus and his Spirit they help accomplish that union. Thus, the sacraments help us remember our past, aid us in celebrating our present life with the Lord and point to our future life of perfect union with the Father in eternity.

The following chart provides a brief summary of this section of the chapter. It gives an overview of the seven ritual sacraments and their relationship to key moments in our lives as well as the particular values of Jesus they celebrate.

SACRAMENT	LIFE EVENT	VALUES OF JESUS
baptism	birth	conversion; accepting the good news
confirmation	growth	strength of the Spirit to live a committed Christian life of service
Eucharist	daily life together; meal	strength of unity to live a life of love
reconciliation	sin and guilt	forgiveness and reunion with the community
anointing of the sick	sickness and near-death	healing and strength to endure
holy orders	service, vocation	ministry of love to God's people
marriage	vocation, family life	ministry of love to spouse and children

EXERCISES:

A. *Bible Research.* Our definition of the ritual sacraments indicated that the sacraments are traceable to Jesus' acts and words as he dealt with people in their time of need. Below are several New Testament passages. Read to discover which sacrament they point to, and explain briefly which value is symbolized in the passage.

New Testament passage	Sacrament	Values
1. Mt 9:35-36 Mt 28:16-20	_____	_____ _____

2. Jn 6:47-58 _____   _____
   Lk 22:14-20
                                 _____

3. Jn 2:1-11 _____   _____

                                 _____

4. Lk 12:8-12 _____   _____
   Jn 16:5-16
                                 _____

5. Lk 7:36-50 _____   _____
   Jn 20:19-23
                                 _____

6. Mk 8:22-26 _____   _____
   Mk 1:40-45
                                 _____

7. Mt 3:13-17 _____   _____
   Mt 16:15-16
                                 _____

B. *Prayer and You.* Our definition of the seven sacraments said that the sacraments are part of the ritual of the church, the public worship the church offers to God. Public worship is public prayer. But, as you well know, Christians are called upon to pray in private as well. Jesus did so often by withdrawing to the hills and to the desert. He expects his followers to pray as well. (See Mt 6:5-15.) Examine your own prayer life. First, read the Matthew passage listed above and Lk 11:1-13. Then complete the following statements by circling the response that best describes your prayer life:

1. I pray: daily   weekly   monthly   rarely

2. When I pray: I do it alone   I do it with others   I don't

3. When I pray and ask for something: I expect my prayers to be answered   I don't expect an answer

4. The last time I really prayed was _____

5. My last prayer: asked for something   thanked God   praised God   asked for forgiveness

6. I pray: before meals   after meals   upon rising in the morning   when I go to bed

7. My experience of prayer is   very good   good   fair   boring

8. When I pray, I usually do it in this place: _____

9. I want to make the following resolution about prayer for this coming week:

Question: Why is prayer essential for those of us who wish to be "sacraments" of Jesus?

C. *Jesus' Values and You.* Our discussion of the sacraments stressed that they reflect the values of Jesus. Are Jesus' values your values? Check the appropriate column for each value. Then, with your classmates, find an example from the New Testament where Jesus demonstrated this value.

	A strong point with me	I'm pretty good at this	OK	I need work	New Testament passage
patient when mis-understood					
love children					
in touch with nature					
concern for the individual					
compassionate—identify with others' feelings					
strong when standing up for the truth					
trustful of others					
prayerful					
forgiving					

SUMMARY

To understand sacramental reality, one must begin with the fact that people can create and use sumbols and signs that have meaning beyond themselves. Most anything can be a symbol to which meaning is attached. The important thing to remember is that we men and women are symbolic beings who both discover and attach meaning to symbols.

A sacrament is a special kind of symbol. It is a sign of God's love for us, his mystery of salvation. It is a sign that brings about what it points to and points to what it brings about.

In a special way Jesus is the first sacrament. His humanity is the sign of God with us. (See diagram below.) The church is the sacrament of Jesus. The members, the body, point to the head, Jesus. Each individual Christian has his or her role to play in making Christ present in the world today. The seven sacraments are signs given by Christ which help us grow closer in friendship to God. They are grace-filled moments that commemorate the Paschal Mystery, demonstrate the reality of Christ in the world today and point to our future union with the Father in his kingdom.

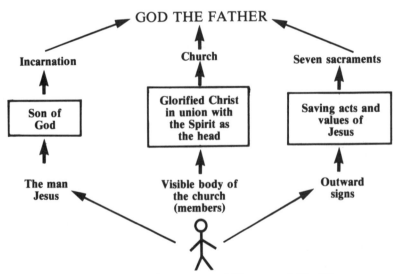

Diagram 1: The Sacramental Nature of Reality

EVALUATION

To test your understanding of this chapter, write a short essay explaining the meaning of the diagram above. Be sure to discuss the following points in your essay:

1) definition of a sacrament

2) the role of Jesus

3) the role of the Christian

4) the function of the seven sacraments

ADDITIONAL EXERCISES

1. Interview Assignment.

Try to discover how a person from another Christian religion understands the term "sacrament." Do so by interviewing the person. If possible, arrange a meeting with a Protestant minister. List points of similarity and points of difference in relation to the ideas presented in this chapter.

2. Reading Assignment.

Read a short biography of a saint or some other "hero" who demonstrated in his or her life that God makes a difference.

3. Creative Projects.

a. Make an audio tape of some music that helps you feel closer to God. Share this music with your classmates and explain how the music helps you think of God.

b. Make a list of your favorite television shows or movies. Discuss how the values in shows or movies either reflect the values of Jesus or contradict his values.

c. Research the meaning of one of the most important Christian symbols—the cross. Find out the answers to these questions:

(1) What did a cross mean to a Roman citizen in the year A.D. 20? Why?

(2) What did St. Paul mean when he wrote, "The language of the cross may be illogical to those who are not on the way to salvation, but those of us who are on the way see it as God's power to save" (1 Cor 1:18)?

(3) What might the horizontal bar of the cross symbolize? the vertical bar?

3

Baptism—Entrance Into the Christian Community

(You are) All baptized in Christ, you have all clothed yourself in Christ, and there are no more distinctions between Jew and Greek, slave and free, male and female, but all of you are one in Christ Jesus. Merely by belonging to Christ you are the posterity of Abraham, the heirs he was promised.
—Gal 3:27-29

Some of the most familiar words in all of the New Testament are those Jesus said before he ascended into heaven. As Matthew puts it:

> Meanwhile the eleven disciples set out for Galilee, to the mountain where Jesus had arranged to meet them. When they saw him they fell down before him, though some hesitated. Jesus came up and spoke to them. He said, "All authority in heaven and on earth has been given to me. Go, therefore make disciples of all the nations; baptize them in the name of the Father and of the Son and of the Holy Spirit, and teach them to observe all the commands I gave you. And know that I am with you always; yes, to the end of time" (Mt 28:16-20).

These words are the Lord's commission to his disciples to carry on his work on earth: to baptize and to teach in his name. Baptism, along with confirmation and the Eucharist, is a sacrament of Christian initiation. These three sacraments incorporate a person

61

into the church and enable the person to share in the mission of the church. As the American bishops have recently stated, baptism and confirmation make it possible for the Christian to share in Christ's priesthood (*National Catechetical Directory, #115*). This chapter will take a closer look at baptism, the first sacrament of initiation. After an introductory section, the chapter will focus on some of the major symbols used in the sacrament, then move on to a discussion of adult baptism and the infant baptism with which most of us are familiar. The chapter will conclude with some comments on how to live out the baptismal commitment. Chapter 4 will then treat the sacrament of confirmation while Chapter 5 will discuss the very important sacrament of Christian unity, the Eucharist.

INTRODUCTION

Please consider the following common human situations. A young couple brings home from the hospital a newborn baby. The husband has put up a welcome sign for his wife and new child. He makes dinner for his wife. Family and friends come over and shower the baby and proud parents with gifts. It is an exciting day for parents and child alike. Or take your older brother who has gone off to college. Within a few months he has written home and told the family that he has joined a fraternity. In the letter your brother recounts some crazy things he had to do to be accepted into the fraternity. You consider the various pranks a little "out of it" but are willing to shrug your shoulders and smile at the apparent joy of your older sibling.

Let's take a few more examples. A family moves into your neighborhood. Your mother welcomes them by preparing a dinner; your father invites the parents over for some socializing. Your family's welcoming the new neighbors reminds you of when you moved into the neighborhood: the apprehension of not knowing what to expect mixed in with the excitement of a new house.

Do you remember what you did when you got your driver's license? When you graduated from high school? If those events are still in your future, how do you plan to celebrate them?

All of these events seem unrelated, but they really involve some common elements: some new (and perhaps exciting) event which took some preparation has taken place; this event demands some kind of celebration. In a sense they all involve a kind of initiation, too. For example, graduation from high school results from a lot of hard work. It represents completion of a stage in your life. But it also initiates you into adult society where you are no longer just a "teenager"; you are now a "young adult." This demands some kind of celebration. Your brother experienced the same thing when he was accepted into the fraternity. He passed the initial tests and the fraternity celebrates by throwing a party for the new "pledges." So, too, the young husband and wife who waited and worried for nine months rejoice at the arrival of their new baby. The worry and work demand some kind of celebration to welcome the infant into the family.

Baptism is somewhat like these common events of life. It is a sacrament where new life is celebrated. At the same time, especially for adults, it comes after a period of preparation, after some time spent considering what the reception of the sacrament will mean to the individual (just like the family which had to consider all the consequences of its move to a new home). Finally, it initiates the individual into the community. It is a sign of God's welcome and the welcome of the Christian community. Just as the driver's license or diploma grants you certain rights and duties, so does baptism also grant the new Christian all the rights and responsibilities of a member of Christ's body. Baptism, then, is an initiation ceremony and a celebration. It confers responsibilities and rights and demands some kind of preparation. Keep these ideas in mind as we begin our discussion of this sacrament. But first, consider the following exercises.

Exercises:

A. Make a list of three clubs or organizations to which you have belonged which required some kind of "initiation rite." Briefly describe the rite, exercise, test or familiar experience you had to undergo in order to be accepted into the group. For example, what activities were associated with being a Boy or Girl Scout? Or what physical skills did you have to demonstrate to "make" a particular athletic team?

Organization	*Initiation Rite*
1. _____	_____
2. _____	_____
3. _____	_____

Discussion:

a. Share the experiences you mentioned above with your class-mates. Do you see any common elements in them?

b. Are there any groups to which you definitely do *not* want to belong? Why? Is it because the personal sacrifice you have to make is too demanding for what you would get out of participation in the group? Is it because you definitely do not like what the group stands for? If yes, explain. Is it for some other reason?

c. Do you think that a group worth belonging to should have some requirements before an individual is accepted into the group? Why or why not?

B. Catholics are a group of Christians who expect their members to believe and do certain things. Below are listed some of these beliefs and practices. How do you live up to them? Rate yourself using the following scale:

    4 — I definitely believe this or live it

    3 — Most of the time this reflects my belief or practice

    2 — I make an honest effort to believe this and live it, but I fall short quite often

    1 — I don't believe or practice this

Beliefs:

_____ I believe in the doctrine of the Trinity: There is one God with three persons—Father, Son and Holy Spirit.

_____ I believe Jesus Christ is God, that he suffered and died for me and all people, that he lives and cares about me.

_____ I accept Jesus' forgiveness and the fact that he is my personal friend and savior.

_____ I believe that the Catholic church was founded by Christ; is one, holy, catholic and apostolic; and I accept the pope as Christ's representative on earth.

_____ I believe in the communion of the saints and that one day I will rise in glory to be with God the Father in union with Jesus and the Holy Spirit for eternity.

Practices:

_____ I make an effort to pray every day, to share with those less fortunate than I and to sacrifice (for example, by fasting).

_____ I attempt to live the Ten Commandments and the Beatitudes; that is, I try to love God above all things and my neighbor as myself.

_____ I live with a set of values, an ethical standard, stricter than society's.

_____ I consider all people my brothers and sisters in Christ and try to act toward them in this way; this includes my enemies, the poor, the lowly, etc.

_____ I see a definite connection between the way I believe and how I treat others.

_____ I celebrate the Eucharist with the Christian community on Sunday and I believe that Jesus is present in the Eucharist.

_____ I confess serious sins at least once a year and receive Communion during the Easter season.

_____ I see a connection between my belief in the Lord and my attitudes and practices concerning sex.

_____ I support my church financially and defend it against unjust attacks.

_____ I am willing to tell people that I am Catholic and to share the good news of Jesus.

Discussion:

1. Add up your ratings for the previous exercise. What total do you think should be required to be a member of good standing in the Catholic church? Was your total above or below that mark?

2. Should the church require its members to believe in certain things and act in a certain way? Why or why not? How would Jesus answer this question?

3. Make a list of issues on which societal and gospel values differ. Do you have any suggestions on how these differences can be resolved?

BAPTISMAL SYMBOLS

For us to appreciate the rich meaning of the sacrament of baptism, it is necessary to reflect on the meaning of some of the symbols used in the baptismal ceremony.

List as many uses as you can think of for the following symbols. Then, as a class, see how many different responses you came up with for each symbol. Discuss which of the uses are positive ones, which are negative.

1. water: _____

_____

_____

2. oil: _____

_____

_____

3. fire: _____

_____

_____

_____

Water and the Spirit. The most important baptismal symbol is water. What does water make you think of? If you are of a scientific mind, you may have written the symbol H_2O. Perhaps you answered that water quenches thirst and thus gives life. It makes plants grow. It cleanses us, our clothes and the things we use. On the other hand, you may have mentioned that water is sometimes a destructive force. Floods, torrential rains, destructive tides represent the awful force of water. Both good—like cleansing rains and cool drinks—and evil—like shark-infested seas or polluted rivers—are associated with water. Water is one of those universal symbols that carries rich meaning. It has been adopted in the sacrament of baptism by the church to represent some realities of our initiation into the Christian community. The meaning of water in the sacrament of baptism relies heavily on both Old Testament and New Testament sources. Let us turn to some of these scriptural "fountainheads" of the sacrament.

1. *Old Testament.* Water meant both destruction and life for the Jew. In Genesis (1:1-2), water is described as the primeval chaos, a hostile element. The story of the great flood in Noah's time prompted the Psalmist to petition Yahweh:

> Save me, God! The water
> is already up to my neck;
>
> I am sinking in the deepest swamp,
> there is no foothold;
> I have stepped into deep water
> and the waves are washing over me (Ps 69:1-2).

This passage clearly describes the destructive force of water.

But the Old Testament depicts God's power as bringing life through water. God's spirit hovering over the watery chaos in Genesis was responsible for the order of creation. The waters of the Red Sea saved the fleeing Jews from the pharaoh at the time of the Exodus. In the 40-year sojourn in the desert, the Jews were refreshed with water from a rock. Joshua crossed the waters of the Jordan River and led the exiled Jews to a land "flowing with milk and honey." Time and again the Old Testament writers describe water as life-giving and renewing. Witness this quote from Ezekiel:

> Then I am going to take you from among the nations and gather you together from all the foreign countries, and bring you home to your own land. I shall pour clean water over you and you will be cleansed; I shall cleanse you of all your defilement and all your idols. I shall give you a new heart, and put a new spirit in you; I shall remove the heart of stone from your bodies and give you a heart of flesh instead (Ez 36:24-26).

The quote from Ezekiel brings together in a beautiful way the theme of water and the Spirit. God's Spirit is associated with water as in Genesis when it is God's breath (*ruah* or Spirit) which dries the lands. The wind (*ruah*) blowing from the ocean brought with it water and coolness, refreshment and rain. It came to be associated with the life-giving breath and saving waters of God who cared for his people.

The ancient Jews also used water in their rituals. They used water to cleanse believers from impurities. They also had a kind of baptism for Gentile converts to Judaism. Converts were baptized in Jordan's waters to symbolize their entry into the freedom of the Promised Land.

2. *New Testament.* Water was used in John the Baptist's ritual baptism. His baptism called for people—both Jews and Gentiles—to turn from their sins forever in expectation of God's kingdom. John's baptism was followed by serious demands that the baptized live their lives in accordance with God's law. Thus, it meant death to an old life of sin and a conversion to a new life of expectation of the Messiah.

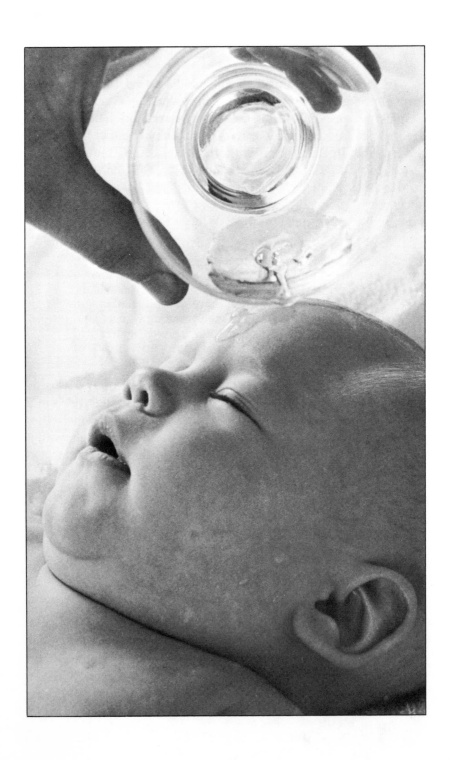

Water and the Spirit also have an important role to play in Jesus' baptism by John the Baptist. (See, for example, Lk 3:21-22.) The theologian Bernard Cooke asserts that Jesus' baptism symbolized three things: that Jesus is the *new Israel,* the *new Adam,* and the *Messiah* (Christ). First, Jesus, though without sin, freely entered the Jordan River to symbolize that a new era had begun. Just as the Jews had passed into the Promised Land through the Jordan, Jesus passed through the waters of the Jordan to indicate that through his passion and death we will arrive at the Promised Land of salvation won by his resurrection. Second, just as the Genesis account had God bringing human life out of the watery chaos symbolized in the creation of Adam, the baptism of Jesus tells us that God (symbolized by the dove) has created a new life, a new humanity through his Son, Jesus. Third, the Jews had waited for the fulfillment of the promises of the Messiah, he who would restore Israel to its rightful place among the nations. At Jesus' baptism we hear the words: "You are my Son, the Beloved; my favour rests on you" (Mk 1:11). Jesus accepted his commission and ushered in the new age of God's salvation. Note again how water and the Spirit (symbolized by the dove) converge at the baptism of Jesus.

Besides symbolizing the fact that Jesus is the new Israel, the new Adam and the promised Messiah, Jesus' baptism is a prefiguring of his passion, death and resurrection. Jesus' descent into the waters of the Jordan with all their potential to destroy pointed to his passion and death. But when he emerged from the waters, there was a pointing to his resurrection, to new life. God's Spirit is poured out on Jesus at his baptism just as his Spirit is given to the Christian community after his resurrection from the dead.

3. *Baptismal Waters Today.* This rich symbolism of water and the Spirit is evident today when the Christian is baptized. To be baptized is to go into the destructive waters which signify that we have died to evil and sin and rise with Jesus to be anointed with his Spirit. To say it another way, the one who is baptized "converts" or turns from sin to begin a new life with the Lord. St. Paul stresses this point when he says that the baptized are no longer slaves to sin but slaves to God (Rom 6) and that we put off the old

man and put on the new (Col 3:9). This dress imagery was symbolized in the early church by the baptized person undressing before entering the baptismal waters and dressing again in a white robe when he or she emerged with Christ. In today's baptismal liturgy a white cloth is given to the infant to remind us of our transformation in Christ. Finally, the water used in baptism suggests a new birth through the action of the Spirit. The person is initiated into the Christian family. As an interesting aside, some of the early baptismal fonts were in the shape of a womb to suggest that the waters of baptism were like the waters that surrounded the baby in the mother's womb.

Exercises:

1. Have you ever felt the destructive forces of water? its life-giving properties? What did you think at the time of your experiences? Were life and death prominent in your mind?

2. *Reading deeper.* Check out the following scriptural passages and discuss how they fit into the discussion of the symbolism of water treated above.

Ex 17:3-7	Ez 47:1-9,12
Rom 6:3-5	1 Cor 12:12-13
Rv 22:1	Ps 23:1-4
Jn 4:5-42	

Fire. One of the most fascinating universal symbols is fire. Perhaps it is so fascinating because it combines both beauty and danger; it draws us near, yet frightens us away at the same time. One of the important lessons of childhood is learning that the beautiful flame hurts if one gets too close.

Even with the wonders of electricity and other forms of energy, people love fireplaces and campfires. There is nothing quite like a warm fire on a cold winter's night. And gathering around a campfire is one of the prime symbols of human fellowship and friendship.

1. *Old Testament.* For the ancient Israelites, fire stood for the presence of God. You might recall that Yahweh appeared to

Moses in the middle of a burning bush (Ex 3:5). When the Israelites wished to picture God's presence among them, they spoke of the cloud of Yahweh covering the tabernacle by day and fire covering it by night (Nm 9:16). For the Jews, God was fire because without him they felt lost in a dark night. Also, fire gives the appearance of being alive but without a fixed or final form. The living God Yahweh is alive but always free and unpredictable. Finally, fire is all-consuming. Nothing can survive its intense heat. So, too, the Jews rightly believed that God's love is irresistible and all-consuming.

2. *New Testament*. The New Testament speaks of fire symbolically, too. For example, John the Baptist says to the crowds about Jesus, ". . . but the one who follows me . . . will baptize you with the Holy Spirit and fire" (Mt 3:11). In addition Jesus says this about his mission: "I have come to bring fire to the earth, and how I wish it were blazing already!" (Lk 12:49).

One of the most important characteristics of fire is that it gives light. Jesus used light imagery extensively in his teaching about himself. John's Gospel not only images Jesus as the Passover lamb and the manna in the wilderness but as the pillar of fire: "I am the light of the world; anyone who follows me will not be walking in the dark; he will have the light of life" (Jn 8:12). We confess in our creed at Mass that Jesus is light that came into the world and that he is light from light. Those who don't recognize Jesus prefer the darkness of sin to the light of Christ.

A second important characteristic of fire is warmth. Love and affection are sometimes spoken of as "warm." Loving people are sometimes described as having "warm" personalities. It is the Spirit of Jesus and his Father who warms people's hearts with love. On Pentecost Sunday the Spirit was represented as tongues of fire which descended on the apostles who were to preach and live the love of Christ. Acts records the founding of the church this way:

> When Pentecost day came round, they had all
> met in one room, when suddenly they heard what
> sounded like a powerful wind from heaven, the

noise of which filled the entire house in which they were sitting; and something appeared to them that seemed like tongues of fire; these separated and came to rest on the head of each of them. They were all filled with the Holy Spirit, and began to speak foreign languages as the Spirit gave them the gift of speech (Acts 2:1-4).

3. *Fire and baptism.* What does fire have to do with baptism? Well, in the baptismal liturgy, after being clothed with the white garment symbolizing the new Christian dignity of being clothed with Christ, the newly baptized Christians are given lighted candles. At that time the following prayer is recited:

Receive the light of Christ. Parents and god-parents, this light is entrusted to you to be kept burning brightly. This child of yours has been enlightened by Christ. He (she) is to walk always as a child of the light. May he (she) keep the flame of faith alive in his (her) heart. When the Lord comes, may he (she) go out to meet him with all the saints of the heavenly kingdom.

What this means is that a new Christian is to be the light of Christ, shining before men and women so that they can see Christ working in the world. The new Christian is to burn with the love of Christ, with the love of Jesus' forgiveness and service to all. His or her vocation is to be a beacon that points to the good news of Jesus.

The Oil of Christ. The rite of baptism for a child includes two anointings with holy oil. The first takes place before baptism and the second takes place immediately after the pouring on or immersion into the baptismal waters. With the second anointing with the holy oil, called *chrism,* the celebrant says:

God the Father of our Lord Jesus Christ has freed you from sin, given you a new birth by water and the Holy Spirit, and welcomed you into his holy people. He now anoints you with the chrism of salvation. As Christ was anointed Priest, Prophet, and King, so may you live always as a member of his body, sharing everlasting life. Amen.

The holy oil used in baptism is an important symbol with profound meaning. Before we discuss the interpretation of this symbol recall what you wrote about its uses. Perhaps you noted that oil is used in cooking; without it, many of our foods and salads would taste quite bland. Oil is also an important ingredient in many cosmetics and medicines. For example, think about the agony sunbathers would suffer without its soothing effects. Athletes in the ancient world (and weight lifters today) used it to lubricate their bodies before contests. In today's world, oil is vitally important as a fuel and as a lubricant for machinery, as well as playing an essential part in the production of plastics, fertilizers and many other goods. Our whole economy is tied to its availability. Without it, the Western world would grind to a halt. In a real way today, oil is *the* symbol for wealth.

1. *Biblical meaning of oil.* In scriptural times olive oil was mixed with an aromatic substance called balsam. It was used to anoint. For example, balsam-perfumed oil was used to anoint the heads of guests at dinner parties to show respect and esteem. You might recall from Luke's Gospel how the Pharisee Simon failed to extend this courtesy to Jesus, but the notorious woman who was a sinner rushed in from off the street to do so (Lk 7:36-50). Dead bodies were also anointed with oil as a preparation for burial. This was the task the women went to perform on Jesus' body Easter Sunday morning (Mk 16:1).

The Jews also used to consecrate their altars and priests with holy oil to symbolize God's sweet, continuous presence. But the most important use for oil in biblical times was the anointing of kings by either priests or prophets. One of the most striking examples of this is David's anointing by Samuel as described in 1 Samuel, Chapter 16. In time, anointing of the king—God's servant or son—took on special significance. In Israel there arose a belief that a special "anointed one" of God would come at the end of time to overcome the world. The title *Messiah* meant "anointed one" and designated this anointed redeemer.

Christians, of course, believe that Jesus is the "anointed one of God, the Messiah." His anointing by God's Spirit was pictured at his baptism. His mission was foretold in Isaiah. Here, the Messiah was not seen as a glorious king to be served by the nations of man, but as a Suffering Servant. Read the marvelous words of the prophet:

> Here is my servant, whom I uphold,
> my chosen one in whom my soul delights.
> I have endowed him with my spirit
> that he may bring true justice to the nations.
>
> He does not cry out or shout aloud
> or make his voice heard in the streets.
> He does not break the crushed reed
> nor quench the wavering flame.
>
> Faithfully he brings true justice;
> he will neither waver, nor be crushed
> until true justice is established on earth
> for the islands are awaiting his law (Is 42:1-4).

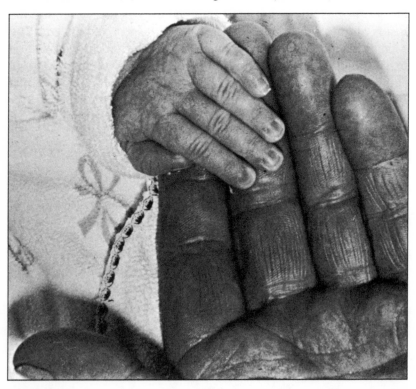

2. *Anointed With Christ.* When the Christian is anointed with chrism, he or she takes on Christ. "Christians" get their name because they are anointed followers of the Anointed One, Jesus Christ. (*Khristos* is the Greek word for "Messiah—Anointed One.") Each Christian is called on to be another Christ, to share in his role of Suffering Servant for all peoples. Baptism is sometimes called "christening" to underscore this reality. The rich symbolic anointing with chrism reminds the Christian that his or her task is to walk in the footsteps of Jesus. It stresses symbolically that to be anointed with Jesus Christ means to serve as Jesus served, to wash the feet of others as Jesus demonstrated (Jn 13:1-17).

A. *Further research.* Jesus came to serve, not to be served. To get a truer picture of the kind of Messiah Jesus was, read the Suffering Servant Song, Isaiah 52:13-53:12. Make a list of the various descriptions that directly apply to Jesus. Also, read Jn 13:1-17 and discuss its significance.

B. *Prophet, Priest and King.* As the prayer at the baptismal anointing suggests, the Christian shares the prophetic, priestly and kingly mission of Jesus, the mission defined by his life and teaching. Here is an essential Christian definition for each term:

Prophet: one who speaks the truth even in the face of persecution; one who proclaims God and speaks for him

Priest: an intermediary between God and humans; one who offers true worship to the Father

King: one who rules by serving others

Each Christian is called to live his or her prophetic, priestly and kingly vocation. Below are listed a number of activities which a follower of Christ might perform. Decide which role is manifested in the given activity.

_____ praying the Our Father

_____ tutoring students in an elementary school

_____ receiving the Eucharist

_____ working for a pro-life amendment

_____ regularly contributing to the missions

_____ apologizing after insulting someone

_____ thanking God for the gifts of life and faith

_____ sticking to principles and not going along with others in doing wrong

How can you live your role as (1) prophet, (2) priest, and (3) king in your life as a young person? (Share examples of persons who have lived this role in your life.)

1. _____

2. _____

3. _____

C. *Your name.* At baptism, you were given two names. The important name you acquired when you were anointed with chrism. There you received the name "Christian"—one who is anointed in Jesus Christ. This name gave you the privilege and responsibility to live as a prophet, priest and king just as your namesake Jesus did.

But you received a second name, too. At the very beginning of the baptismal liturgy the priest asked your parents, "What name do you give your child?" *Ordinarily,* parents choose the first name of a Christian saint for their child. In a special way, this saint's example should serve as a guide for the new Christian who has joined Christ's body.

Write your baptismal name here: _____

As a brief research project, find the answers to these questions:

a. What does your Christian name mean?

b. Tell some facts about this saint's life.

c. What qualities of your namesake do you especially admire?

d. List and then discuss the significance of other baptismal names sometimes given to children; for example, Faith, Hope, Grace, etc.

You may wish to consult various lives of the saints for this project. An important resource is *Butler's Lives of the Saints.* If desired, do an extra credit report discussing in more depth questions b and c above.

ADULT BAPTISM

In the early church, baptism for adults was the norm. A person desiring Christian baptism did so undoubtedly because he or she was attracted to the Christian community—a group of people who were known for their amazing lifestyle. St. Luke wrote this about the early Christians: "The whole group of believers was united, heart and soul; no one claimed for his own use anything that he had, as everything they owned was held in common" (Acts 4:32).

Let's say that you lived in the first century and had a pagan friend who wished to become Christian. What would he or she have to do? Generally, you would have to sponsor your friend. Your sponsorship insured that your friend would willingly live a Christian lifestyle and give up anything that was contrary to Christian belief. The period of watching out for your friend was called the *catechumenate* and usually lasted three years. During this period, the *catechumen* learned about the Christian faith and lived a life of prayer, fasting and conversion. The commitment to become a Christian was very serious because Christians were a hunted group in the first century and were subject to persecution and even martyrdom. A catechumen had to know exactly what his or her choice involved.

The baptism itself took place on Holy Saturday after a 40-day period of prayer and formal instruction in the faith. During this period the candidate would learn the creed and the Our Father. From what St. Justin Martyr and others wrote in the second century, the baptismal service had the following dimensions:

- The candidate prayed and fasted on Holy Saturday to prepare spiritually for the baptism.
- The church community prayed and fasted with the candidate to demonstrate that baptism was not an isolated event but a community celebration.
- The candidate was questioned by the bishop to see if he or she was really ready for baptism and knew what the commitment meant.

• The candidate promised to give up Satan and his evil ways.

• The bishop "sealed" the candidate with oil. This "sealing for Christ" recalls St. Paul's phrase of becoming an athlete for Christ, ready to struggle for the good news. After this first anointing, the candidate entered the water. Baptism was by immersion to signify dying and rising with Christ.

• The candidate was asked the three trinitarian questions: "Do you believe in the Father? Do you believe in the Son? Do you believe in the Holy Spirit?"

• After the candidate emerged from the water, his or her five senses were anointed with chrism and all prayed that the new Christian be filled with the Spirit. (This part of the ceremony is now called confirmation.)

• The candidate was given a new white garment as a sign of new life in Christ. A candle lit from the Easter candle was given to symbolize that the new Christian was filled with the light of Christ.

• The new Christian was introduced into the assembly, common prayers were said, the kiss of peace was given and the Eucharist was celebrated. At the eucharistic celebration, the newly baptized would receive his or her first Holy Communion.

Adult Initiation Today. In 1972, the church issued an important document entitled the *Rite of Christian Initiation of Adults.* Its purpose was to restore the ancient practice of adult baptism with all its rich symbolism. The document shows a sensitivity to the need for preparation of adults for baptism in missionary lands. It also serves as a reminder that mature adult faith is needed to be a Christian in today's world. *The new rite demonstrates an awareness that getting baptized just because it is the "thing to do" or having infants baptized in a setting where their faith will not have a chance to grow is not sufficient reason for welcoming a person into the Christian community.* Baptism demands a "turning away" from sin and a life lived in harmony with the demands of the Gospel of Jesus. The new rite should help Christians realize that Christianity takes mature commitment and sustained effort.

This rite has a lot in common with the way baptism was performed in the early church. First, the current rite for adults is rather elaborate and includes all the sacraments of initiation: baptism, confirmation, Eucharist. Early Christians thought of these sacraments as a unit. Only later were they separated, with another sacrament—penance—added.

Second, we can see that the early form of baptism included all the symbols so beautifully highlighted in today's baptismal liturgy: oil, candle, white cloth, water, the trinitarian creed. Their inclusion in the Easter Vigil points to the great Christian feast of Easter which celebrates Jesus' triumph over sin and death. Today, the rite for adults normally takes place on the Easter Vigil just as it did in the first century.

Third, both the ancient baptismal liturgy and the revised rite for adults stress the community aspect of initiation. The community is active in sponsoring, instructing, praying, greeting and welcoming the candidate. These aspects are highlighted in the new rite to show that every Christian needs the support, friendship and love of his or her fellow Christians in living out the baptismal commitment in a sometimes hostile world.

Finally, the new rite has restored the catechumenate which was taken quite seriously in the early years of the church. The revised rite sees the catechumenate in four stages: (1) The candidate inquires about the faith and has the good news preached to him or her. (2) The candidate enters the order of catechumens and is instructed for a period of time, maybe several years. At the end of this stage, the candidate is *elected,* that is, chosen to be a Christian because he or she has demonstrated the sincerity of his or her faith. (3) This stage takes place during the Lent prior to baptism and includes a period of prayer, fasting and penance to ready the person for baptism. (4) There is a final period during the Easter season after baptism when the new Christian gains spiritual fruit and enters more closely into the life of the community. Through all of these stages, the sponsor plays an active part supporting the candidate.

Reflecting on the new rite for adults and the early form of Christian baptism should drive home to us that baptism into the Christian community is serious business. Christian life demands commitment. It demands that we know that to follow Christ means to turn from sin and live a life of love and service. It means that we are willing to suffer with Jesus.

THINGS TO DO:

A. *A DEBATE:* Some people think that baptism should be administered *only* to adults. Their essential argument is that Christianity is an *adult* religion and thus takes adult faith and commitment. Do you agree? Divide the class into two groups: one that favors baptism for adults only, another that holds for the traditional practice of baptizing infants. Using current articles from religious periodicals, find reasons to support your side of the debate. Write several of the reasons for both sides in the space provided. What conclusion did your class reach in the debate?

Adults only   *Infant baptism*

1. _____   1. _____

   _____   _____

2. _____   2. _____

   _____   _____

3. _____   3. _____

   _____   _____

4. _____   4. _____

Conclusion: _____

B. Interview your parish priests and ask them if the *Rite of Initiation for Adults* has been used in your parish. If so, ask the following questions:
   1. How long was the catechumenate?
   2. What role did the sponsors play?
   3. When did the baptisms take place? Where?
   4. Did the parish community participate in the preparation and instruction of the candidates? How did the community celebrate with the newly baptized adults?

C. *Visit* another Christian denomination. Ask the minister how baptism is handled in his or her community. Or interview a rabbi and ask him how initiation is practiced in the Jewish community.

D. *Scriptural Reflection.* Baptism has to do with rebirth, turning away from a life of sin and acceptance of a new life with Jesus. As a class, read aloud the following important scriptural passage: Woman at the Well (Jn 4:1-30). Pause briefly and reflect on the passage. Then respond to the following questions.

1. If I had witnessed this passage, I would have (circle one):

   a. been confused

   b. wondered who this Jesus was

   c. been amused at Jesus' ability to read hearts

   d. desired some of the water of which Jesus spoke

2. If I had been in the shoes of the Samaritan Woman, I would have:

   a. probably ignored what Jesus said

   b. asked for living water

   c. run to tell my friends that I had found the person who took away all my fears

   d. listened to what Jesus said but not have understood him

3. In my own words, this scriptural passage means:

E. *Personal Reflection:*

   1. Would you sponsor a friend for baptism? Why or why not?
   2. Would you sponsor yourself for baptism? Why or why not?

INFANT BAPTISM

How did your debate on the merits of infant baptism turn out? Did you conclude that baptism is best reserved for adults because it demands faith, maturity and commitment? If so, you may wonder why the church baptizes infants.

Scholars admit that in the first century very little was said about infant baptism. A mention of baptism usually meant adult baptism. However, there are references to whole households being baptized. When parents converted to Christianity, they tended to have their children baptized, too. By around the year A.D. 500, though, the entire Roman Empire was virtually Christian. From that time on infant baptism became the custom.

How can infant baptism be justified? Several reasons are offered. The first has to do with the long tradition of infant baptism. In the introduction to the *Rite of Baptism for Children* we read that "from the earliest times, the church to which the mission of preaching the Gospel and of baptizing was entrusted has baptized children as well as adults" (no. 2). This argument from tradition is not conclusive because not everyone agrees that we should continue to do something just because "we always did it this way."

A second reason stems from the theology of St. Augustine and the doctrine of original sin. Augustine was writing against the heretic Pelagius who denied that we need God's grace to attain salvation. Augustine reacted by saying that we are born into a world tainted with sin, and that the effects of this sin prevent people from reaching God by their own efforts. We need God's grace. For example, we need the graces of the sacrament of baptism to help us on our journey through life to the Father.

Relying heavily on a gospel passage about the necessity of rebirth through water and the Spirit (Jn 3:5), Augustine went so far as to say that unbaptized infants who die are unable to see God face-to-face in the afterlife. Today, theologians basically dispute this view because they believe that God's infinite mercy extends the effects of Jesus' saving deeds to those infants who die unbaptized.

Nevertheless, in the *Rite of Baptism for Children* the Sacred Congregation for Divine Worship insists: "An infant should be baptized within the first weeks after birth. If the child is in danger of death, it is to be baptized without delay" (no. 8).

Third, infant baptism effectively symbolizes God's unconditional love. It is a reminder to the Christian community that God takes the initiative; it does not depend on us—our maturity, our ability to think, what we have done. God's love extends to us simply because we are. This reason is appealing. In both his letters to the Romans and to the Galatians, St. Paul reaffirms this point. Paul writes that nothing we do can claim salvation; it is by God's grace, through faith, that we are saved. But there is a possible objection here: Are infants capable of faith?

The way to reflect on this question of faith is to look at baptism not as an individual thing meant only for the recipient. Rather, we should look at baptism in the context of Christian community. By baptizing the infant, the Christian community is saying that we have faith. Our faith is important to us. Our faith is something we wish to share with and demonstrate to the child. We have certain values like cleanliness, kindness, respect for life. But our most important value is the value of the good news of Jesus. We want to care for the child in our faith community so that one day the child will make our faith his or her faith. Of course, the final decision whether to accept and live the implications of his or her baptism rests with the grown child. He or she can never be forced to accept God's free gift of love and friendship. The child can only be shown by a loving community that God's love is so important and dynamic that the community wishes to share it with the child from the very beginning.

One ought to look at baptism of infants, then, as a community celebration and a community commitment. It is a *celebration* because the community rejoices in God's great gift of love which he extends in baptism. Baptism is a free gift that even our children can benefit from. Baptism is also a community *commitment* because the baptism of a child reminds the Christian community that it has the obligation to live the good news of Jesus so that the growing child can experience the love of Christ. By letting Christ's light shine through, the community hopes that one day the child will accept Christ's love for himself or herself.

QUESTIONS:

1. List at least five things your parents value. Gather your list by asking them what they value as well as by your own observations.

   a. _____   d. _____

   _____   _____

   b. _____   e. _____

   _____   _____

   c. _____

   _____

   Are any of the five related to the good news of Jesus?

2. Are you glad your parents baptized you a Catholic? Why or why not?

3. At this point in your life, how would you answer the following:

   a. To me, being a Christian means _____

   _____

   b. To me, being a Catholic means _____

   _____

4. After rating yourself on the following items, share your responses with a classmate. 1—means very strong agreement; 2—agree; 3—undecided; 4—disagree; 5—strong disagreement.

   a. I am proud to be a Catholic.

   |____|____|____|____|____|
     1   2   3   4   5

   b. I believe in the good news of Jesus.

   |____|____|____|____|____|
     1   2   3   4   5

c. I would be willing to suffer for my faith. (For example, I would put up with being laughed at to express my beliefs.)

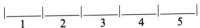

d. I am willing to tell others about my faith.

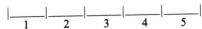

e. If the occasion should arise, I would die for my faith.

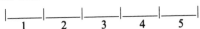

5. If you were the pastor of a parish, what kind of faith commitment would you demand of parents seeking baptism for their child? Check any of the following which you would require. Explain your choices.

_____ parents go to Mass weekly

_____ parents say they will educate the child in the Catholic religion

_____ parents support their church financially

_____ parents attend two classes on the meaning of baptism

_____ parents participate in parish life beyond attendance at Mass

_____ parents' marriage is stable

Other: _____

_____

_____

_____

THE RITE OF BAPTISM FOR CHILDREN

For your convenience, here is a brief summary of the ritual of baptism for one child.

1. **Reception of the Child.** Baptism should take place on Sunday. The parents and godparents present the child for baptism. In the name of the Christian community the priest greets all present and reminds them of the joy of the occasion. After the parents tell the priest that they want the child baptized, the priest says:

> You have asked to have your child baptized. In doing so you are accepting the responsibility of training him (her) in the practice of the faith. . . .

II. **Celebration of God's Word.** An appropriate gospel passage is read (for example, Mt 28:18-20, Rom 6:3-5, Gal. 3:26-28) after which the priest explains what baptism is about. Various prayers of the faithful are recited. The priest then prays for the child and anoints him (her) with the oil of exorcism. He prays:

> We pray for this child:
> set him (her) free from original sin,
> make him (her) a temple of your glory,
> and send your Holy Spirit to dwell with him (her).
> (We ask this) through Christ our Lord.

III. **Celebration of the Sacrament.** The priest blesses the water. Then he asks the parents and godparents in the name of the child to reject sin and make a profession of faith. What follows is the actual baptism.

A. *Baptism.*

> Celebrant: I baptize you in the name of the Father,
> and of the Son,
> and of the Holy Spirit.

B. *Anointing with Chrism.* The child is anointed on the crown of the head.

C. *Clothing with the White Garment.*

> Celebrant: See in this white garment the outward sign of your Christian dignity.

D. *Lighted Candle.*

> Celebrant: Receive the light of Christ.

E. *Prayer over Ears and Mouth.*

> Celebrant: The Lord Jesus made the deaf hear and the dumb speak. May he soon touch your ears to receive his word, and your mouth to proclaim his faith, to the praise and glory of God the Father.

IV. Conclusion of the Rite.

> Celebrant: Dearly beloved, this child has been reborn in baptism. He (she) is now called the child of God, for so indeed he (she) is. In confirmation he (she) will receive the fullness of God's Spirit. In holy communion he (she) will share the banquet of Christ's sacrifice, calling God his (her) Father in the midst of the church.

All join in to recite the Our Father after which the priest blesses the mother, then the father and finally the entire congregation. His final words are a petition

> Celebrant: May he (God) send his peace upon all who are gathered here, in Christ Jesus our Lord.

PROJECT:

To make this chapter more meaningful, participate in a baptismal ceremony and then write your reactions to it in your journal. Possibly either you or a classmate will have a relative who will be baptized soon. You might arrange to have the class go to the celebration.

LIVING YOUR BAPTISM

Most of us were baptized as infants. In a way, the decision was made for us by our parents and godparents. They wished us to be members of God's family from the very beginning of our life. Does this mean we have no choice in the matter?

We should look at baptism as more than just a single event that took place in our life many years ago. The Fathers of the church at the Second Vatican Council had this in mind when they wrote:

> But baptism, of itself, is only a beginning, a point of departure, for it is wholly directed toward the acquiring of fullness of life in Christ. Baptism is thus oriented toward a complete profession of faith, a complete incorporation into the system of salvation such as Christ himself willed it to be, and finally, toward a complete participation in Eucharistic communion (*Decree on Ecumenism, #22*).

In reality, baptism is something we live every day. We have the free choice of whether or not we want to be members of the Christian community. Our choice involves saying yes to Jesus' command to love.

Every time we struggle to resist the temptations of sin, we are saying yes to Jesus. Every time we go out of our way to help parents, friends, brothers and sisters, even strangers, we affirm our baptism. When we pray and when we sacrifice for others we strengthen our commitment. When we worship our God with the Christian community we are in truth saying that we want to belong and that we care for our brothers and sisters in Christ.

When we do these things we make our baptism truly ours. We shine with the light of Christ which we were given as infants. We let the world know that we are proud to be called "Christian," anointed ones of the Anointed One. We know it is a struggle at times, but a struggle worth the effort because we proclaim that we belong to Christ as he belongs to us. The question each of us must ask ourselves is: Do we want to belong to Jesus Christ?

QUESTIONS:

1. How do *you* live your baptism?

2. Do you belong to Jesus Christ?

SUMMARY

1. The sacraments of initiation—baptism, confirmation and the Eucharist—incorporate the Christian into Christ's body and enable him or her to share in the priestly, prophetic and kingly mission of the church.

2. The symbols of baptism speak of the following realities:
   a. *Water* points to our rebirth in Christ, our death to sin, our purification as we enter the Christian community. It symbolizes total transformation.

   b. The *fire* of the candle reminds us to let the light of Christ shine through. It symbolizes Christ's all-consuming love.

   c. The holy oil, called *chrism,* reminds us that we have taken the name *Christian* and are followers of the "Anointed One."

3. The norm of baptism in the early church was adult baptism. The revised *Rite of Christian Initiation for Adults* highlights many of the same elements found in the earliest baptismal ritual: the extended catechumenate; the community support; baptism on the Easter Vigil; the symbolism of water, oil, white cloth, candle, the trinitarian creed, etc. The earliest initiation ceremony saw baptism, confirmation and Communion as a unit.

4. Today infant baptism is the custom. The practice relies on a long tradition, on the free gift of God's love which is

needed to help Christians attain salvation in a sin-filled world and on the Christian community's commitment to share its gospel values with the new child.

5. We recommit ourselves to our baptism daily when we follow the Lord's direction and example.

EVALUATION

Imagine that a friend asks you to sponsor her for baptism as a Catholic. What would you tell your friend about what is to take place and what it means?

ADDITIONAL EXERCISES

1. **Creative Project.** Do one of the following:

   a. Make a banner to be used at a baptism. Include on it symbols that represent what takes place at baptism.

   b. Design a "baptismal certificate" which relates what has taken place in baptism for the new Christian.

   c. Select some appropriate songs to be used at a baptismal ceremony.

   d. Make a slide presentation on the symbolism of light and water.

2. **Research Project.** Do one of the following:

   a. Obtain a missal and read the prayers recited at the Easter Vigil. Write an essay describing how the Holy Saturday liturgy uses baptismal themes. Outline the service.

   b. Research how Buddhism, Hinduism or Judaism uses water, fire and oil in its worship services.

   c. Attend a Greek or Russian Orthodox or an Eastern Rite baptism and report differences from and similarities to Roman Catholic baptism.

   d. Research what the Baptists believe about infant baptism.

   e. From the rite and interviews with priests, parents and godparents, list the responsibilities of a baptismal sponsor.

3. **Project.** Volunteer your service in planning for a baptism at your parish. For example, your parish youth group could plan a reception—party—to celebrate the baptism.

4

Confirmation—
Strengthening Commitment

Let us leave behind us all the elementary teaching about Christ and concentrate on its completion, without going over the fundamental doctrine again: The turning away from dead actions and towards faith in God; the teaching about baptisms and the laying-on of hands; the teaching about the resurrection of the dead and the eternal judgement. This, God willing, is what we propose to do.

—Heb 6:1-3

The second sacrament of initiation is confirmation, which means "making strong" or "strengthening." In confirmation the work of our baptism is "strengthened" or "completed." The quote at the beginning of this chapter gives a scriptural basis for the sacrament of confirmation. The Letter to the Hebrews lists among the first elements of Christian instruction both the teaching about baptism and the laying-on of hands. "Laying-on of hands" is considered by the church as the true beginning of the sacrament of confirmation.

Confirmation is a much-discussed sacrament today as the church debates what theological emphasis should be put on the sacrament. For example, some people stress that the original order of the sacraments of Christian initiation—baptism, confirmation, Eucharist—is the norm and should be restored in sacramental practice. Others focus on confirmation as the entry into Christian maturity or Christian adulthood. Still others stress that confirmation completes the initiation into full membership in the Christian community, regardless of age or personal maturity.

Some of these concerns will be treated in this chapter. After our opening exercise, the chapter will very briefly treat the history of the sacrament so that the different emphases of today can be understood better. Then the theology of the sacrament will be discussed, followed by a treatment of what age is best for confirmation. There will be a section on the ritual of confirmation, and the chapter will conclude with a few considerations on the meaning of confirmation in your life.

Before we look at the history of the sacrament, please do the following exercise on maturity.

EXERCISE: Confirmation has been called the sacrament of maturity. In what sense is this meant? Certainly, it has nothing to do with psychological or physical maturity. It does *not* initiate a person into physical adulthood, nor does it say that the confirmed person necessarily has his/her "act together." Rather, in confirmation God calls the Christian to a more mature life of Christian responsibility. It is a call to live a more mature response to God's love, the love first experienced at baptism. For this reason, some say baptism and confirmation belong together.

Confirmation helps us become more mature spiritually. The question is: How spiritually mature are you at this stage of your life? Below are listed several signs of spiritual maturity. Check your spiritual maturity "quotient" by marking the following chart.

Spiritual Maturity Quotient

The spiritually mature person	This is me....		
	most of the time	sometimes	rarely
• prays often			
• is not afraid to witness to his/her faith			
• goes it alone if necessary in doing the right thing			
• shows concern for the poor			
• willingly learns about his or her religion			
• asks for God's forgiveness			
• admits when he or she is wrong			
• makes Jesus central in life			
• actively participates in the liturgy			

QUESTIONS:

1. Define maturity: _____

2. Who is the most mature person you know and why did you select him or her?

3. Is a person ever really mature or is maturity a process? Discuss.

HOW MATURE AM I?

Adolescence is a period of life when young people "ripen"—mature. Here is a list of possible traits of a mature adult. Check those which you think you show most of the time. Compare your list with a close friend and discuss how you might grow.

The mature person

____ objectively observes what happens around him or her

____ accepts his or her physical traits

____ has a sense of humor

____ is patient

____ has friends of the opposite sex

____ accepts the complexity of life

____ appreciates and befriends people of different ages

____ likes to learn

____ is curious about other people and places

____ hates violence and respects life

____ occasionally prays

____ doesn't blame others when things go wrong

____ enjoys some work

____ recognizes that life is a gift

____ is simple but not simpleminded

____ is sensitive to people

____ accepts trials, setbacks graciously

____ sometimes likes the formality of weddings, graduations, etc.

____ appreciates his/her own talents

____ sometimes acts "goofy" to balance out overseriousness

____ is courageous when sick

____ accepts death

_____ gets along with others, but likes solitude, too

_____ goes out of way to help others

_____ accepts changes in self and others

_____ recognizes and practices self-discipline

Add other traits here:

_____

_____

_____

SHORT HISTORY OF THE SACRAMENT OF CONFIRMATION

It is worthwhile to take a brief look at the history of confirmation to better understand some of the debates over the sacrament today.

Period 1 (first to fifth centuries). In the early church what we today call confirmation was united with the baptismal liturgy of the Easter Vigil. You might remember from the last chapter that in the first century of the Christian era, the adult member was initiated into the Christian community after a long period of preparation. The baptism took place on the Saturday before Easter and included a number of symbolic actions.

Let's review the sacramental actions in the early initiation rite: 1) The candidate renounced Satan. 2) A priest anointed the candidate for a first time. 3) A deacon led the candidate to the baptismal pool. 4) The three baptismal questions were asked. 5) After the person was baptized and emerged from the pool, another anointing took place. 6) White garments were put on. 7) The new Christian then entered the church. 8) The bishop then laid on hands, prayed for the Holy Spirit and its gifts and anointed the new Christian with the oil of thanksgiving. 9) The bishop kissed the new Christian and welcomed him/her into the community. 10) After the kiss of peace was shared with the congregation and the prayers of the faithful, the Eucharist was celebrated. At this time the newly adopted child of God received Holy Communion for the first time.

All these actions constituted the liturgy for receiving new members into the early church. What we now call confirmation was part of the liturgy and specifically included the laying-on of hands, the anointing by the bishop and the prayer for the Holy Spirit (see eight above).

This ancient practice of the church has been restored today and is called the Rite of Christian Initiation for Adults. During this Eastertime ceremony, converts receive the sacraments of baptism, confirmation and Eucharist simultaneously as they are welcomed into the church. Including confirmation stresses the intimate connection between the sacrament and initiation into the community.

Period 2 (6th to 20th centuries). When the church was numerically small, it was possible for the bishop to be present at each baptismal ceremony. But when the church grew in numbers, the bishops were unable to be present in all their parishes for the initiation ceremonies. However, the bishops wished to retain some role in the ritual of initiation. Thus, around the sixth century, they began to reserve for themselves the right of anointing after baptism and the various prayers for the coming of the Spirit. As leaders of the Christian community and the successors of the apostles, they wished to "confirm" the initiation of the candidates. Gradually, then, confirmation was separated from the baptismal ceremony so the bishop could administer the sacrament at a later time.

As Christianity spread so did the custom of infant baptism. By the 13th century church leaders saw a need for youngsters to learn about their baptismal commitment. Confirmation became a logical event for catechetical instructions and an opportunity for young people to say "yes" to the faith they received at baptism.

Confirmation, then, was administered usually to young people from the ages 7 to 12. (In 1566, the Catechism of the Council of Trent stated that after baptism confirmation should be given to all, but that it was best to wait until children reached the age of reason.) However Holy Communion was not received until around age 14. The ancient order of receiving the sacraments—baptism/confirmation/Eucharist—was retained, but they were administered over a span of years rather than in one ceremony.

Period 3 (20th century). Perhaps you were confirmed in the seventh, eighth or ninth grade. Your parents were probably confirmed in the fifth or sixth grade. But most of you and your parents were confirmed *after* first Holy Communion. Why this change from Period 2? In the early part of this century (1910), Pope Pius X wished to foster devotion to the Eucharist, and he made it possible for Catholics to receive Communion when they reached the age of reason (around seven years of age). He believed that once a child knew the difference between ordinary bread and wine and the consecrated bread and wine (the body and blood of Christ) the child should not be deprived of the special help and closeness to the Lord given in this sacrament. So, for most of us who were baptized as infants, confirmation was administered after first Holy Communion.

Today. As we look at the history of this sacrament we can conclude that the time of its administration has changed over the centuries. But today, people are debating just when confirmation should be celebrated. Some think that we should go back to the way it was done in the early church. As a matter of fact, the Eastern Catholic churches do allow priests to baptize, confirm and give Communion to infants. Others argue solely for adult baptism and want to retain the ancient order of administering the sacraments of initiation. Still others, who stress the theme of confirmation as the sacrament of Christian maturity, want the sacrament delayed until a much later time, perhaps either late high school years or early adulthood (19-25 years of age).

When should confirmation take place? What do you think? Before formulating an answer, read the next section of the chapter which discusses some of the theology of the sacrament, and which might influence your decision.

SOME EXERCISES:

Discuss:

1. At what age were you confirmed? Was this a good age for you? Why or why not?

2. List some things you remember being taught about the sacrament of confirmation.

IMPORTANT SCRIPTURE ASSIGNMENT:

Confirmation—besides being called the sacrament of Christian maturity—is in a unique way the sacrament of the Holy Spirit. At confirmation the bishop lays hands on the candidate, anoints the forehead with chrism and recites the important words: "Be sealed with the Gift of the Holy Spirit." Sealing in the Holy Spirit binds the confirmed Christian to spread, defend and witness to the faith in both word and deed.

But who is the Holy Spirit and what influence does he have on the Christian? Read the following scriptural passages on the Holy Spirit and briefly state the main point of the passage.

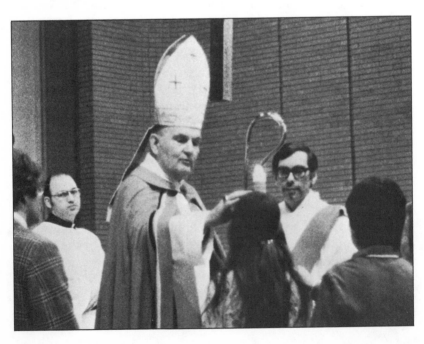

What the Bible Says about the Holy Spirit

I. *The Promise of the Holy Spirit in the Old and New Testaments*

Reference	Summary
1. Is 61:1-3,6,8-9	
2. Ez 36:24-28	
3. Jl 2:23; 3:1-3	
4. Jn 14:15-17	

II. *The Coming of the Spirit*

1. Acts 2:1-6	
2. Acts 19:1-6	
3. Mk 1:9-11	

III. *The Role of the Spirit*

1. Rom 5:1-2, 5-8	
2. Rom 8:14-17	

IV. *Gifts of the Spirit*

1. 1 Cor 12:4-13	
2. Gal 5:16-25	

V. *Responsibility of the Christian in Response to the Spirit*

1. Eph 4:1-6	
2. Mt 16:24-27	
3. Jn 14:23-26	

MORE ON THE GIFTS: One of the main functions of the sacrament of confirmation is to celebrate the gifts of the Holy Spirit. The traditional list of the gifts of the Holy Spirit is found below. Briefly define each gift and then give an example of how you have used or can use that gift in living out a Christian life. (See 2 Pt 1:3-8.)

Gifts	Definition	Example
Wisdom		
Understanding		
Knowledge		
Counsel		
Fortitude		
Piety		
Fear of the Lord		

Your Gifts: 1 Cor 12:4-13 stresses the fact that the Holy Spirit gives different gifts to each Christian, though the purpose of the gifts is to build up the body of Christ. The theme of the gifts of the Holy Spirit is "unity in diversity." What are your gifts? The following exercise is designed to help you discover the special gifts or talents which have been given to you to serve others.

What are my gifts?

    A—This description fits me most of the time. (I seem to have this gift.)

    B—This describes me *some* of the time.

    C—This doesn't seem to be me.

_____ 1. When someone is having a tough time, I can cheer the person up.

_____ 2. I communicate what's on my mind well.

_____ 3. I know when someone is hurting.

_____ 4. I'm an optimist. (I tend to say a glass is half filled with water rather than say it is half empty.)

_____ 5. I'm willing to take risks.

_____ 6. I'm a good listener.

____ 7. I'm a hard worker who sticks to a task.

____ 8. I accept cheerfully what happens to me.

____ 9. I respond with compassion when others suffer misfortune.

____ 10. I'm a leader.

____ 11. I'm not afraid to challenge an irresponsible statement.

____ 12. I would be willing to die for someone or something I believe in strongly.

____ 13. I genuinely like to learn.

____ 14. I seek advice for difficult decisions and make decisions thoughtfully.

____ 15. I value friendships more than money.

____ 16. I understand and respect others' opinions.

____ 17. I pray often.

____ 18. I do not fear change and new challenges.

____ 19. I accept people as individuals and reject others' stereotypes.

____ 20. I can handle disappointments.

FOLLOW-UP: Discussion and Reflection.

A. Write a 50-word "personal profile." Stress your special gifts.

B. Write a prayer or poem thanking God for the special gifts he has given you. Mention a definite commitment to use your gifts for others in the next week.

C. As a class, discuss what specific gift each of the 20 statements above represents.

D. What attitude should we as "gifted people" have?

E. Can you think of a song title that reflects your "specialness"? If so, write it here:

_____

_____

F. Of the gifts of the Spirit—wisdom, understanding, knowledge, counsel, fortitude, piety, fear of the Lord— is there one you have ignored in yourself, or have not recognized fully?

G. What kinds of tasks and responsibilities could the Lord depend on you to do?

THE MEANING OF CONFIRMATION

As an introduction to this section, study the following chart. Derived from the "General Introduction to Christian Initiation" as found in the *Roman Ritual,* it attempts to distinguish the different effects of the sacraments of initiation.

Effects of the Sacraments of Initiation		
BAPTISM	CONFIRMATION	EUCHARIST
• makes us members of Christ's body • forms us into God's people • remits sin (both original and personal) • makes us a new creation as adopted children of God	• seals us with the gift of the Spirit • makes us more Christlike • gives us strength and courage to give public witness to our faith • gives us desire to do the Spirit's work: preach the good news of Jesus	• provides spiritual food for our pilgrimage to God • acts as a sign of the unity of God's people • serves as a sharing in the sacrifice of the cross, leading to redemption • offers ongoing opportunity to ask God for the Spirit to move people's hearts to accept Jesus as Lord

Do you notice any similarities? The outstanding common trait of these sacraments is the freeing of the Christian from the power of darkness—sin. In short, baptism brings with it a *new birth*—a turning from sin—an initiation into God's family, Christ's body. Confirmation *strengthens* the initial commitment by giving the fullness of the Spirit and his gifts so the Christian can live fully the responsibilities assumed at baptism: responsibilities to be Christlike, to witness to and defend the faith. The Eucharist *con-*

tinually renews the baptismal-confirmation commitment by giving us the person of Jesus himself to free us from sin, to bind us into a fervent community and to help us in our Christ-given command to preach and live the good news.

Let us turn briefly to three themes that will help us understand the sacrament of confirmation.

Theme 1: *Confirmation is a deeper initiation into the faith community.* Scripture provides a foundation for this theme:

> When the apostles in Jerusalem heard that Samaria had accepted the word of God, they sent Peter and John to them, and they went down there, and prayed for the Samaritans to receive the Holy Spirit, for as yet he had not come down on any of them: they had only been baptized in the name of the Lord Jesus. Then they laid hands on them, and they received the Holy Spirit (Acts 8:14-17).

The significance of this passage is that the early church recognized a deeper immersion into the Christian community, one that went beyond baptism. In the words used at confirmation, this immersion is called "sealing."

What does it mean to be sealed by the Holy Spirit? To be sealed means "to belong to." In ancient times some people wore seals around their necks to show they belonged to someone. Kings sealed their documents with an official stamp to show others that the contents of the documents came from them. Today we brand animals to communicate the same kind of meaning.

In confirmation the Christian is given the *fullness* of the Holy Spirit. The Spirit's presence fully incorporates the Christian into the community of believers. Using words like "sealing" and "fullness" relates confirmation to baptism. In baptism the Father adopts us as his children—his family (the People of God) becomes our family through the power of Jesus' Spirit. In confirmation the Holy Spirit comes to the family member offering the grace and gifts necessary to live a true Christian identity.

Stressing confirmation as a sacrament of initiation underscores the close relationship between the Son and his promise that the Father will pour out the Holy Spirit on the believers. By keeping in mind that confirmation *initiates* us into Christian life, we will not easily forget that the Father who adopts us through his Son Jesus at baptism pours out the Spirit of love at confirmation.

Theme 2: *Confirmation celebrates the gift of the Holy Spirit and the gifts he bestows on us.* Confirmation not only results in a deeper membership in God's family, it bestows on the believer the gift of the Spirit. The words of the sacrament highlight this point: "Be sealed with the gift of the Holy Spirit."

To have the gift of the Holy Spirit enables the Christian to live a courageous life in response to God. How does the Spirit manifest himself in your life? Here are a few examples of when the Christian might experience the presence of the Holy Spirit: when we have hope against terrific odds; when we carry out our responsibilities, even though our efforts don't seem to have much promise of success; when we faithfully accept death; when we experience love, beauty, joy; when we put up with the petty goings-on of everyday life; when we pray in silence knowing that there is a God who listens to us and cares for us; when we see a setback as an opportunity to learn; when we turn our doubts and despairs over to God; when we simply know that God loves us even when many are against us. Each of us can surely add to this list of times when God's abiding presence (the Holy Spirit) comes to help, sustain and reassure us. It is this Spirit whom we celebrate in confirmation.

Theme 3: *Confirmation is the sacrament of witness.* Before the current rite of confirmation was renewed, those receiving the sacrament received a ceremonial slap on the cheek. Some people mistakenly thought that this slap symbolized the abuse a Christian was going to have to take for witnessing to his or her faith. Historically, though, the slap was similar to the pat on the back a parent might use in sending a child to do a task. Athletes use similar kinds of gestures to encourage their teammates in a game.

A gesture of peace has replaced the ceremonial slap, but the idea behind the gesture remains: it calls and encourages the Christian to give more serious witness to God's saving love for all people.

Jesus gave us his Spirit to help us live the kind of life that makes his death and resurrection believable to people today, to strengthen us to proclaim our faith to the world, and to call Jesus our own and to share in the work of bringing all people to the Father.

The Spirit gives each of us special gifts to complete this task whether we do it alone or with others, whether we do it by speaking out or by being silent.

When you refuse to go along with the crowd or challenge a cruel remark, when you resist the temptation of sex and drugs or you openly discuss your faith with others, then you are witnessing to the Lord. You are critiquing values prevalent in society that are contrary to your values as a Christian.

SOME EXERCISES:

1. In your journal, write a brief essay recounting a time you felt the special presence of the Holy Spirit in your life. For example: the special strength to continue after a setback; the joy of a special achievement; the courage to do the right thing in a trying situation. As a witness to the good news, share these essays with your classmates.

2. *Christian heroes:* In today's confirmation ceremony, candidates are not required to take a special name. Rather, the baptismal saint serves as the candidate's special guide. Likewise, confirmation no longer requires a special sponsor. Parents or the baptismal sponsor are now preferred. The confirmed Christian should look to the saint and to the sponsor for inspiration on how to live a life of witness.

a. Write a short essay on how your sponsor or parents have witnessed to their faith. You may wish to interview them for this assigment.

b. If you did not research the life of your patron saint in the last chapter, do so now and write a brief report on how he or she witnessed to Jesus Christ.

c. Select another saint or a contemporary Christian hero who especially inspires you. Briefly report on his or her life and explain why you admire the person. Here are some possibilities:

Mary, the Mother of Jesus	Mother Teresa of Calcutta
St. Francis of Assisi	Dom Helder Camara
St. Ignatius Loyola	Damien the Leper
St. Catherine of Siena	Thomas Dooley
St. Therese of Lisieux	St. Elizabeth Ann Seton
(The Little Flower)	Martin Luther King
Pope John XXIII	A priest or religious
Dorothy Day	Some other admirable
A parent	person

3. *Christian witness.* The Apostolic Constitution on confirmation says: "Having received the character of this sacrament, they (the confirmed) are 'bound more intimately to the church' and 'are strictly obliged to spread and defend the faith both by word and by deed as true witnesses of Christ.' " As a class, construct a list of things you can realistically do to spread the faith by word and by deed. Here are some starters:

By word	By deed
• teach religion to younger students	• support the missions
• discuss your religion with friends	• resist peer pressure which might compromise your doing the right thing
• write pro-life letters to newspapers	• visit old folks
	• assist "special" children or take part in a Big Brother or Big Sister program.

4. *A confirmation debate.* Now that you have read some re-flections on both the history and the meaning of confirma-tion, divide the class into five groups. Present arguments in the form of a debate on which age is best for the reception of this sacrament. These are the five age groups.

    1. In infancy (with baptism) or when an adult is bap-tized

    2. Between the sixth and ninth grades

    3. Between the 10th-12th grades

    4. As a young adult (ages 19-25)

    5. As a mature adult

5. Let's say you had a 15-year-old daughter whose friends are being prepared for confirmation. Your daughter doesn't seem at all interested or ready for the sacrament. Would you "force" her to take confirmation classes? Why or why not?

THE AGE FOR CONFIRMATION

How did your debate on the best age for confirmation turn out? There is probably no right answer to this debate—a debate that will be with us for a long time. Undoubtedly, the age decided on will vary from diocese to diocese and even from parish to parish. It really depends on which factor tends to be emphasized. Here are some of the emphases in the church today.

1. *Psychological readiness.* Some people stress confirmation as the sacrament of maturity. In our contemporary world, adulthood is delayed until a person has finished college or begun a career. At this time real decisions are made. If this is true about or-dinary life, some say that confirmation should be delayed until a

person is old enough to really appreciate the deeper commitment to Christianity he or she is making, and can intelligently and freely decide to renew the commitment made for him or her at baptism.

2. *Traditional argument.* Others argue that confirmation is a free gift of God's grace and should not depend on psychological readiness. For one thing, a person is never mature, only maturing. They say, for example, that it is certainly OK to confirm a sixth-grader because the child is aware of the special help the Holy Spirit provides even at that young age.

They argue that confirmation gives a "sacramental character"—the person goes through a public, official sealing by the Holy Spirit through the bishop who represents the Christian community. The grace of confirmation marks the Christian who now has a full and certain relationship for his/her future life in the church. At any point in the future, the young Christian can call on the fullness of the Spirit to help him/her live out the demands of the Christian life.

3. *Liturgical reasons.* Some emphasize the history of the sacrament and take the traditional arguments one step further, and argue that there is no reason confirmation cannot immediately follow baptism, even for infants. They stress confirmation as a sacrament of initiation. "Why not fully initiate the young Christian into the community?" they ask. There is historical precedent for doing so, and the Eastern churches have maintained the ancient tradition. Here—it is true—one would sacrifice the role of the bishop, but he could certainly extend his full symbolic value of initiation into the community.

FOR REFLECTION:

A. Interview a priest or director of religious education in your parish and ask at what age confirmation is administered there. Ask what theological reasons and diocesan policies undergird this practice. Share your findings.

B. *Another reason.* A traditional argument for confirming at a later age is that it gives the young Christian another chance to receive formal religious instruction. This is especially important for those who do not go to Catholic schools and are in religious education programs. If confirmed as infants they might not have the chance for further instruction in the faith. What do you think of this argument? Is it realistic knowing that many would not attend further religious education classes after reception of first Holy Communion and first penance? Or is it a poor excuse and merely using the sacrament as a kind of "carrot on a stick" to force attendance at religion classes? Debate this point in class.

C.   *Mini-research topic:*

Charismatic Catholics—those who testify to the special power of the Holy Spirit in their lives—and other Christians who call themselves "charismatic" use the phrase "baptism in the Holy Spirit." What do they mean by the term? What is its relationship to the sacrament of confirmation? Invite a charismatic to class to explain what is meant by the term.

D.   *"Taking Stock of Your Commitments"*

Take a personal inventory of your commitment to Jesus and the Christian community. As a confirmed Christian, you have the following gifts that you have been given to use to help others:

a. hard work	g. personal sacrifice
b. patience	h. standing alone
c. love	i. criticism from others
d. your life	j. trust
e. time	k. responsibility
f. money	l. faith

Here are some stocks you might invest in. Which of the above gifts (stocks) are you willing to spend? Mark the appropriate letters in the spaces below.

_____ helping to end pollution	_____ going to Mass an extra day each week
_____ tutoring handicapped children	_____ getting involved in the parish youth group
_____ spending time with a lonely classmate	_____ showing offense when someone swears
_____ doing extra chores at home	_____ reading the Bible daily
_____ staying off pot and booze	_____ paying close attention in religion class
_____ being extra nice to brothers and sisters	_____ getting involved in school activities
_____ writing legislators who are pro-abortion	_____ supporting equal rights for minorities

THE RITE OF CONFIRMATION

If you have been confirmed, you may remember the rite of confirmation. You may recall that it took place within a Mass. The priest wore either red vestments to symbolize the presence of the Spirit or white vestments to symbolize Christian initiation.

If you get the opportunity, try to participate in a confirmation liturgy in your parish this year. One of the new themes is the supportive role of the entire community. Your presence at a confirmation will be a source of strength to your brothers and sisters in Christ who are trying to live a more Christian life.

Another good way to learn about the rite and appreciate your own confirmation is to help prepare others for the sacrament. You may serve as a teacher's aide, help plan days of recollection for the candidates and give testimony to the role of the Holy Spirit in your life. Here is a brief synopsis of the ritual for confirmation:

I. **Introductory Rites.** Today it is the custom to celebrate confirmation within a Mass to stress the relationship among the sacraments of initiation. Appropriate readings are selected for the Liturgy of the Word; for example, Ez 36:24-28, Acts 8:1,4,14-17 and Jn 14:23-26. After the reading of the Gospel the candidates are called to the sanctuary of the church. The sponsors often accompany the candidates, especially if they are children. The focus of the bishop's homily is the role of the Spirit in making the newly confirmed more Christlike and better members of the church. After the homily the candidates and those present renew their baptismal vows.

II. **The Laying on of Hands.** This is the biblical gesture through which the bishop and the concelebrating priests invoke the Holy Spirit. The bishop sings or prays:

My dear friends
in baptism God our Father gave the new birth of eternal
    life
to his chosen sons and daughters.
Let us pray to our Father
that he will pour out the Holy Spirit
to strengthen his sons and daughters with his gifts
and anoint them to be more like Christ the Son of God.

All-powerful God, Father of our Lord Jesus Christ,
by water and the Holy Spirit
you freed your sons and daughters from sin
and gave them new life.
Send your Holy Spirit upon them
to be their helper and guide.
Give them the spirit of wisdom and understanding,
the spirit of right judgment and courage,
the spirit of knowledge and reverence.
Fill them with the spirit of wonder and awe in your
    presence.
We ask this through Christ our Lord.

All: Amen.

III. **Anointing with Chrism.** Each candidate kneels before the bishop. The bishop moistens his thumb with the oil of chrism, makes the sign of the cross on the candidate's forehead and says: "N., be sealed with the Gift of the Holy Spirit."

If there are many candidates, the bishop is assisted by the concelebrating priests. The anointing and the words confer the indelible seal of the Lord and bestow the gift of the Spirit. The bishop then greets the newly confirmed:

Peace be with you.

Response: And also with you.

IV. **Prayer of the Faithful.** The prayers of general intercession have as their theme petitions for the newly confirmed.

V. **Liturgy of the Eucharist.** The Mass continues as usual. The Preface is that of the Holy Spirit and the prayers after Communion recall an aspect of the work of the Spirit. The Mass ends with a beautiful blessing by the bishop:

God our Father
made you his children by water and the Holy Spirit:
may he bless you
and watch over you with his fatherly love.

Response: Amen.

Jesus Christ the Son of God
promised that the Spirit of truth
would be with his church for ever:
may he bless you and give you courage
in professing the true faith.

Response: Amen.

The Holy Spirit
came down upon the disciples
and set their hearts on fire with love:
may he bless you,
keep you one in faith and love,
and bring you to the joy of God's kingdom.

Response: Amen.

May almighty God bless you,
the Father, and the Son, + and the Holy Spirit.

Response: Amen.

TO DO:

1. If you have not done so already, read the scriptural passages cited in the rite above. Discuss them in class.

2. As a class project, pick out at least four hymns or songs that would go well with the above rite. You may wish to use them in the paraliturgical exercise at the end of this chapter.

LIVING YOUR CONFIRMATION

Confirmation both celebrates and helps increase your giftedness in our Lord Jesus. It gives you the strength of the Spirit to live your vocation as a child of God. It gives you the power of the Holy Spirit to live boldly and courageously the kind of life that will make a difference, the kind of life that will point to Jesus working in the world.

We live in a world that wants us to conform. It is a world that wants us to dress the same, buy the same things, act like everybody else. Look around and see what conformity brings. Too many people let others make their decisions for them. Too many people act in all too predictable ways. The question is: Are you like too many people?

Or are you different? Do you realize that you have been given the gift of the Holy Spirit and can live a Spirit-filled life? For example, are you willing to go against the crowd? Do you witness to Jesus? Do you share your faith? Do you defend it? Do you act as though the Lord lives in you? Are you concerned with the poor as Jesus was? Do you defend the helpless as Jesus did? Are you willing to affirm the virtues of purity and the sacredness of the human body?

The answers to the questions in the paragraph above are difficult ones. But the sacrament of confirmation gives us the power of the Spirit to respond in a positive way to them. Our positive response goes a long way in making the Gospel come alive in today's world. By taking up the challenge and the gifts of the sacrament of confirmation, we Christians become real symbols of Jesus. By struggling together with our fellow Christians we can—with the help of the Holy Spirit—make the Gospel come alive and mean something in today's world.

QUESTIONS:

1. List some positive and negative aspects of conformity. Discuss them.

2. Is the Christian called to be different? If so, how might you live at home, at school, at work and at play such that you point to Jesus acting in you and the world?

SUMMARY

1. Confirmation means "making strong." In receiving this sacrament, we are given the fullness of the Holy Spirit, are showered with his gifts, are more fully initiated into the Christian community and are called to be strong witnesses of our faith—to proclaim it, defend it and live it.

2. The important gifts of the Spirit given at confirmation include: wisdom, understanding, knowledge, counsel, fortitude, piety and fear of the Lord.

3. Confirmation is a celebration of the Holy Spirit and his gifts.

4. Over the centuries, the age for the reception of confirmation has changed. At first, confirmation was celebrated with baptism and first Holy Communion. When Christianity grew and infant baptism became the custom, it was administered by the bishop at a later age, but usually before first Holy Communion. In more recent times, it was administered after first penance and first Holy Communion because of the pope's desire for young people to participate in the Eucharist.

5. Today, the debates on the best age for confirmation seem to center around whether the theme of maturity or the theme of initiation is stressed more.

EVALUATION

Pair up with one other student. This is your task: One of you is to play the role of a pastor of a parish. The other is to play the role of a candidate for confirmation who is to be questioned by the pastor to see if he or she is ready to receive the sacrament. The "pastor" should make a list of 10 most important questions that should be asked of such a candidate and then ask the questions. The "candidate" should answer them to the best of his or her ability. After the exercise, grade each other according to the following:

> 5—Excellent questions (answers)
>
> 4—Very good questions (answers)
>
> 3—Good questions (answers)
>
> 2—Needs better questions (answers)
>
> 1—Try again

ADDITIONAL EXERCISES

As a closing exercise, celebrate a prayer service that renews the baptismal/confirmation commitment. Here is a suggested format, but feel free to improve on it.

A PRAYER SERVICE

I.   *Opening Song*—"Come Holy Ghost"

II. *Light the Christ candle*

Reading from the Old Testament: Is 61:1-3, 6, 8-9

Response: Read together Psalm 23, "The Lord Is My Shepherd"

III. *Renewal of Baptismal Vows*

Leader: Do you reject Satan,
and all his works,
and empty promises?

Response: I do.

Leader: Do you believe in God,
the Father almighty,
creator of heaven and earth?

Response: I do.

Leader: Do you believe in Jesus Christ, his only Son, our
          Lord,
          who was born of the Virgin Mary,
          was crucified, died, and was buried,
          rose from the dead,
          and is now seated at the right hand of the Father?

Response: I do.

Leader: Do you believe in the Holy Spirit,
          the Lord, the giver of life,
          who came upon the apostles at Pentecost
          and is given to you sacramentally in confirma-
          tion?

Response: I do.

Leader: Do you believe in the holy catholic church,
          the communion of saints, the forgiveness of sins,
          the resurrection of the body, and life everlasting?

Response: I do.

Leader: This is our faith. This is the faith of the church.
          We are proud to profess it in Christ Jesus our
          Lord.

Response: Amen.

Commitment: Write on a piece of paper a resolution to re-
nounce a particular work of Satan or a positive resolution
promising God and your classmates that you will live your
confirmation. As a symbol of your commitment, put your
resolution around the Christ candle.

IV. *Reading:* Eph 4:1-6
     Share insights into this reading with your classmates.

V.   *Recite the Our Father together*

VI. *Closing Hymn.* Select one your class prepared earlier in the
     chapter. Some examples, "To Jesus Christ, Our Sovereign
     King"; "Holy God, We Praise Thy Name"; "Day by Day"
     from *Godspell,* etc.

5

The Eucharist—
The Lord's Supper

For this is what I received from the Lord, and in turn passed on to you: that on the same night that he was betrayed, the Lord Jesus took some bread and thanked God for it and broke it, and he said, "This is my body which is for you; do this as a memorial for me." In the same way he took the cup after supper and said, "This cup is the new covenant in my blood. Whenever you drink it, do this as a memorial of me." Until the Lord comes, therefore, every time you eat this bread and drink this cup, you are proclaiming his death. . . .

—1 Cor 11:23-26

INTRODUCTION

"Do this in memory of me." Jesus, our friend, brother and savior wants to be remembered! Is this not the wish of everyone who walks the earth—to be remembered? But our Lord is different in that he is not just some vague figure from history that we recall from time to time. We Catholics believe that through the gift of the Eucharist, our remembering Jesus the Lord makes it possible for us to receive him! What an incredible opportunity—to receive one's friend.

Yet, how often people neglect to take advantage of this opportunity. Why is this? Perhaps some people are lazy and just can't muster up the energy to go to Mass. Perhaps others don't really believe what Christians in the Catholic community proclaim about the Eucharist. Or some may find the Mass boring and not worth the effort to find meaning in it. Still others may not understand what is going on. And, let's face it, some Masses lack joy, perhaps because the priest or people are bored. Sometimes liturgies are poorly planned, mechanical and lacking in a sense of community.

These are just some of the reasons people don't adequately appreciate the Eucharist. This certainly wasn't always the case. For example, in the Roman Empire of the fourth century, Christians were put to death if they were caught participating in the ritual we call the Mass. Many fearlessly faced death and defended their actions by saying: "Christians make the Eucharist and Eucharist makes Christians. Without the Eucharist we cannot live."

Would you be willing to die for the opportunity to receive our Lord in the Eucharist? What is it the early Christians believed that made them see something extraordinary taking place at the Liturgy of the Eucharist? This chapter will attempt to answer that question by addressing the following themes: What is the meaning of "Eucharist?" What did Jesus do at the Last Supper and why did he do it? How has the Mass changed through the ages? What do we do at the Eucharist and why? How is the eucharistic meal celebrated today—what are its elements? How can you live the Eucharist in your life? As usual the chapter will have some exercises to help you think about the material you have read. Let us start off with one of those exercises.

SOME THOUGHT PROVOKERS

A. *Eucharist: A Memorial Meal.* The Eucharist is a number of things—a sacrifice, a sacrament, a commission. But above all else it is a memorial meal. This suggests two questions: How do you remember special people and special events in your life? What does a meal mean to you? With these questions in mind, complete the following exercises:

   1. *Remembering:* What do you use (perhaps some symbol) to recall the significant persons or events listed below?

- An absent boyfriend (girlfriend): _____
- Grade school graduation: _____
- A favorite vacation: _____
- A deceased relative: _____
- Your most significant athletic achievement: _____
- A favorite concert: _____
- Your best teacher: _____
- A frightening experience: _____

Share these in class. Do you ever discuss any of these with friends or parents around a dinner table or at lunch?

2. *Meals:* What was the most meaningful meal, supper or banquet in which you participated? Why did you come together? What did you talk about? Did anything special take place at the meal? Why was *this* meal so special? Jot a few notes in the space below.

a. Most significant meal:

_____

_____

e. What was served:

_____

_____

b. Who was there:

_____

_____

f. Topics of conversation:

_____

_____

c. What was the occasion:

_____

_____

g. Why was the meal so special:

_____

_____

d. Who served the meal:

_____

Discuss: Share the description of your special meal with your classmates. Then as a group, list some reasons why these special meals involved more than just the sharing of food. In other words, what else is shared at meals?

B. *The Eucharist and You.* Check off those statements below which describe your attitudes, beliefs or practices about the Eucharist.

____ I believe that Jesus is present in my fellow worshippers at the Mass.

____ I usually find the Mass boring.

____ When I go to Mass, I usually receive Communion.

____ When I go to the eucharistic celebration, I usually attend with family or friends.

____ I believe that Jesus is really present under the form of bread and wine in the Eucharist.

____ I wish I could participate more fully in the Mass by reading, singing, responding more wholeheartedly, etc.

____ I don't fully understand the Mass.

____ To me the Eucharist is a real *celebration*.

____ What bothers me about the Mass is that there are so many phonies there.

____ The Eucharist makes me feel close to God.

____ It would be a great tragedy for me if the government forbade Catholics to celebrate the Eucharist.

____ If I were completely on my own, I would still attend and appreciate the Mass as something important to me.

Share your responses with the class.

THE MEANING OF "EUCHARIST"

What we today call the "Eucharist" has had many names over the centuries. For example, in the first century the Eucharist was also called *eulogy* which means "blessing" (*Berakhah* in Hebrew). This term came from that part of the liturgy where Jesus "blessed" the bread, broke it and gave it to his disciples (Mt 26:26).

Another popular name for Eucharist over the years has been the "Lord's Supper." In the very early years, the Eucharist was also called an "agape." *Agape* is translated "love feast." This term emphasized the unity, sharing and love which the early Christians experienced in their weekly gatherings.

You are quite familiar with the term "Mass," another popular name for the eucharistic liturgy. Let's pause on the meaning of this term. You might recall that the Eucharist was the last sacrament of Christian initiation—the sacrament which fully incorporated the Christian into community. In this sacrament the new Christian received the Lord in his resurrected body under the form of bread and wine. To receive Christ is a tremendous privilege, a privilege reserved to the person of faith who has been instructed in the Christian message and baptized and confirmed into the community.

You might remember from Chapter 3 on baptism that the catechumen (the person learning to be a Christian) received three years of instruction before being baptized. Some of this instruction took place in the eucharistic celebration. The first part of the liturgy corresponded to our Liturgy of the Word with various scripture readings and the homily. But because the catechumens were not yet baptized, they were not allowed to remain for the eucharistic sacrifice—what we call the consecration of the bread and the wine and Holy Communion. Thus, they were "sent out" from the assembly; the Latin word for "sent" is *missa* (Mass), the key word which was a signal for them to leave. Later in the history of the Mass, the liturgy ended with the command, *Ite missa est,* which means, "Go, you are sent" (into the world to love and serve others).

The term *Eucharist,* though, is a much richer term for the celebration of the Lord's Supper than, for example, the word *Mass. Eucharist* means thanksgiving. It is derived from Jesus' words at the Last Supper when he gave thanks to the Father before distributing the cup to his apostles (see Mt 26:27).

What is it we thank God for at the Eucharist? A number of things. For one, the Eucharist is a long prayer of thanksgiving to God for the marvels of creation restored in Christ. We thank God for the seas and mountains, for the sun and stars, for the rivers and the fertile lands. We thank God for the gift of life. Above all else, we thank God for his Son Jesus who has rescued creation from sin and corruption. Jesus' incarnation makes all creation holy. As our Savior who is the firstborn of the dead, Jesus makes us (and all of creation) holy so that we can say, "Father, you are holy indeed, and all creation rightly gives you praise" (Eucharistic Prayer III).

Secondly, we thank God for the new covenant established by Jesus. The old covenant promised a land to the Jews; the new covenant promises eternal salvation and the heaven of the risen Lord to the followers of Jesus. In short, we thank God for his incredible love extended to all men and women everywhere, a love demonstrated by the Son's death on the cross.

Thirdly, we praise and thank God for our exodus from sin, our leaving this world and going to the Father (Jn 13:1), entering into the glory of the Resurrection. Christians thank God for Jesus' passover—for his death, his resurrection and his ascension (his glorification). We thank God for our baptism which delivers us from death and sin, for the true light of Christ who guides us on our journey to the Father, for the bread of life which foreshadows the heavenly banquet. We thank God for the love of his Son who accomplishes all of these things for us.

The Eucharist goes by many names but surely "thanksgiving" describes best what we do when we go to Mass.

_____

TWO EXERCISES

A. *Writing a Prayer of Thanksgiving.* For what are you thankful? Below is a list of people, things and events that evoke gratitude in many people. In the space provided, jot down what it is about that person, thing or event that you most appreciate. Use your particular list to write a short prayer of thanksgiving.

a. Myself: _____   b. A parent: _____

c. A friend: _____   d. Something connected
                                   with school:

    _____   _____

e. A favorite activity: _____

f. Something in nature: _____

g. Jesus: _____   h. Your country: _____

Your Prayer: _____

    Dear heavenly Father, . . .

    _____

    _____

    _____

    _____

B. *Psalms of Praise and Thanksgiving.* Read one of the following psalms. Then, put together a slide package with music or a collage which symbolizes the thanks and praise of God expressed in the psalm.

Psalm   8:   thanks for God's greatness and man's dignity
Psalm   18:   thanks for help and victory
Psalm   29:   praise of God's majesty in a storm
Psalm   41:   thanks after sickness
Psalm   65:   thanks for God's blessings
Psalm 104:   praise of God's creation
Psalm 116:   thanks to God in time of need
Psalm 136:   thanks for God's kindness

JESUS' LAST SUPPER

To understand better the Eucharist we celebrate, it is necessary to know what Jesus did at the Last Supper. This is true because our eucharistic celebration is modeled on what Jesus did and told us to do on Holy Thursday evening. Let's first look at what Jesus did by studying the account in Luke's Gospel. Then, let's see the meaning behind Jesus' actions.

> When the hour came he took his place at table, and the apostles with him. And he said to them, "I have longed to eat this passover with you before I suffer; because, I tell you, I shall not eat again until it is fulfilled in the kingdom of God."
> Then taking a cup, he gave thanks and said, "Take this and share it among you, because from now on, I tell you, I shall not drink wine until the kingdom of God comes."
> Then he took some bread, and when he had given thanks, broke it and gave it to them, saying, "This is my body which will be given for you; do this as a memorial of me." He did the same with the cup after supper, and said, "This cup is the new convenant in my blood which will be poured out for you" (Lk 22:14-20).

1. Jesus celebrated a Passover meal with his disciples.

Jesus shared many meals with his friends—on the road, in the houses of the poor and the rich, with saints and sinners. The meal Jesus ate on Holy Thursday, however, was not an ordinary, everyday kind of meal. The Jewish Passover meal was shared on this particular day. It was a solemn feast, a ritual meal celebrated by the Jews every year in Jerusalem.

Why was this feast so special to the Jews? A bit of Old Testament history is needed to answer that question. Passover commemorated Yahweh's covenant with Moses and the Jews who inherited the land of Israel. It was re-enacted every year to remind each generation of the great deeds God performed for the Jews. A covenant, you might recall, was God's loving promise to be faithful and loving always to his chosen people. His only desire was that his people love him and worship him as the one true God. The Passover celebrated anew the Jewish exodus from Egypt and the countless blessings God showered on the Jewish nation which he rescued from slavery. This feast liturgically re-enacted and renewed the Jewish liberation and their formation as a people. To participate in this feast was to meet again as a people the mystery of God's incredible love.

The Passover meal was filled with symbolism. The host of the meal—in this case, Jesus—recited formal prayers, blessed the food, praised God for all the special things he did for his people and thanked him for his great favors: the gifts of food and drink and the life they symbolize, his rescue of the Jews from the pharaoh's armies, his help in the desert and his delivering them into the Promised Land.

2. Jesus gave new meaning to the Passover meal.

In a few dramatic gestures Jesus invested new and important meaning in this particular Holy Thursday Passover meal. First, he ate it with his friends. This meal summed up the love Jesus showed them during his three-year ministry. It was literally a reminder to his friends that he loved them. Soon he was to undergo on the cross the supreme act of love for them.

Second, he took the unleavened bread and transformed it into his body. (The Jews used unleavened bread at this feast to remind them that God sustained them in the desert with manna and that he rescued them from the armies of the Egyptians. Unleavened bread was used by the fleeing Israelites because they did not have enough time to allow the bread to rise.) Bread—the great symbol for the food that sustains life—was used in the Passover meal to remind the Jewish people that God graciously gives life and keeps it in existence. Jesus took this rich symbol and identified it with himself:

> I am the living bread which has come down from heaven.
> Anyone who eats this bread will live for ever;
> and the bread that I shall give
> is my flesh, for the life of the world (Jn 6:51).

Real life is lived by eating the bread of life. This bread is the Savior who has come to rescue humankind from sin and death, just as Yahweh rescued the Jews in the desert.

Next, he blessed the wine and transformed it into his blood. Wine symbolizes life, too. It is also a sign of joy, a drink that gladdens people's hearts (Psalm 104:13-15). The transformed wine becomes Jesus' blood, the blood of a new sacrifice. *Sacrifice* is a giving to someone; it makes one holy. Jesus gave up his life in obedience to the Father. By so doing he gave to us eternal life, union with his Father. His gift of joy—won by his passion and death—was superabundant life. By drinking of the cup of transformed wine, Christians participate in the great saving deeds of Jesus. True life is ours. As Jesus said:

> He who eats my flesh and drinks my blood
> lives in me
> and I in him.
> As I, who am sent by the living Father,
> myself draw life from the Father,
> so whoever eats me will draw life from me (Jn 6:56-57).

3. Jesus established a new covenant.

The words of Jesus quoted in Luke's Gospel make it quite clear that Jesus established a new covenant with us. On the cross at Calvary, Jesus poured out his life so that we may live. His action was a sacrament, a deep sign of his union with the Father. When we remember Jesus (and he requests that we do remember him and his death), we take part in the Paschal Mystery—we directly share in the great mystery of his life, death and resurrection.

What happens at Mass is the sharing of a new covenant, a new agreement between God and his beloved children. Under the form of bread and wine Jesus is saying to us something like this: "Here I am in your midst—in the life-giving forms of bread and wine. I want to remind you that I am true life and that you can have life if you receive me. I want you to share my body and blood. Consume me so that I can become part of you, enter your life and help you live. I am here as broken bread and wine poured out so that all may live. Here I am for everyone, rich and poor, male and female, young and old, black and white. Here I am as the perfect, total gift. Here I am as a reminder to you to do as I did: give yourself for others. I give you myself under the symbols of life (bread) and joy (wine) so that you can have my life and share my joy. Here I am as your friend who will help you be friends to each other. Here I am simply because I love you. Please love each other.''

THINGS TO DO

A. *Research* how the Jews of today celebrate the Passover meal, called a *seder* supper. Give a report to the class. Or invite a Jewish friend or a rabbi to class to re-enact the seder meal and explain the various symbols used in the ritual. Or celebrate a seder meal in class. Be sure to note the similarities between this meal and the Catholic eucharistic celebration. Also, compare the poetry, creeds, rites, etc.

B. *Some Scripture Work:* Listed below are some meals Jesus ate before and after his resurrection. Read about them and briefly summarize them.

Before the Resurrection:

The Meal	Summary
Mt 9:9-13	_____
	_____
Lk 7:36-50	_____
	_____
Lk 19:1-10	_____
	_____

After the Resurrection:

Lk 24:36-48	_____
	_____
Jn 21:9-17	_____
	_____

For discussion:
1. What do these meals have in common?

2. What is the relationship between them and what Jesus did at the Last Supper?

Thought Provoker: Read the parable about the banquet in Lk 14:15-24. Write an interpretation of it here.

C. *More Research.* Through the ages, many things have been added to the Mass, all of which help us appreciate its meaning more deeply. Make a report on the history of one of the following. Be sure to mention why it is used.

1. Vestments: for example, stole, alb, cincture, chasuble; their colors

2. Candles

3. The altar and tabernacle

4. Sacred vessels: chalice, paten, ciborium, cruets

5. The Mass book

6. Crucifix

7. Incense (at some Masses)

D. How is the Mass celebrated in one of the Eastern Catholic rites; for example, the Melkite or Byzantine Rite? Report to the class.

THE EUCHARIST THROUGH THE AGES

Through the ages, the Eucharist has always been based on what Jesus did and said at the Last Supper. But it has developed over time with different emphases and various customs. It is interesting to take a look at this history.

The Infant Church. In New Testament times, the Eucharist was also referred to as "the breaking of the bread." After worshipping in the Jewish Temple, Christians in Jerusalem would then go to private homes to celebrate the fact that Jesus—the Messiah—had fulfilled the Old Testament prophecies about the promised Savior.

First Century. St. Paul tells us that the Eucharist was also called an *agape,* a love feast or common supper. This supper included the consecration of the bread and wine, the breaking of the bread and Communion. St. Paul also writes in 1 Corinthians, though, that there were abuses at this common meal. For example, some people drank too much. For this reason, and because the numbers of Christians grew, the Eucharist began to be celebrated apart from a common meal.

Second and Third Centuries. In the early days, the celebrant at the liturgy had a lot of freedom to say his own prayers for the Mass. Soon, however, some men became known for their eloquent prayers when leading the celebration. Their prayers were written down and became the standard throughout the Christian world. The earliest example dates from 215 and was composed by Hippolytus. Here is part of one of his prayers:

> We give you thanks, O God, through your dear child, Jesus Christ, whom, in this, the last of all periods of time, you sent to save and redeem us and to tell us what you wanted of us. . . . He did what you wanted him to do, and when he suffered, acquiring thereby a holy people for you, he stretched out his hands to free those who believed in you from suffering. When he was handed over to undergo the suffering he had chosen himself, thereby to destroy death, to break the chains the

devil held us in, crush hell beneath his feet, give
light to the just, make a covenant and manifest his
resurrection he took bread, gave thanks to you and
said . . . (here follow the words of institution).

Fourth through Seventh Centuries. During this time, a number of
things changed in the liturgy. Here are some of them:

- In 384, church leaders decided that the Mass
  should be said in Latin rather than Greek. The
  reason for this change was that most of the people now spoke and understood Latin. (However,
  there have always been rites in the church where
  people were allowed to speak their own
  language, for example, the Byzantine and
  Maronite rites.)

- Much more emphasis was placed on the
  sacrificial aspect of the Eucharist. As a result,
  Eucharist as meal tended to fade into the
  background.

- In the seventh century Pope Gregory the Great
  declared that the Latin Mass in Rome was the
  standard for the Western church. Pope
  Gregory's decree, with some changes made by
  Pope Pius V in 1570, gave the Roman rite its
  basic form until 1964 when Pope Paul VI
  modified it to the Mass we have today.

- People tended to receive Communion less often
  because they heavily stressed Christ's divinity
  and their own unworthiness.

The Middle Ages (Eighth through 15th Centuries). Theologians of
this period debated the meaning of the "real presence" of Christ
in the eucharistic bread and wine. During this period there was a
great stress put on the consecration. The theological term "transubstantiation" was introduced to indicate that the bread and wine
really turned into Jesus' risen body and blood, although the appearance of bread and wine remained.

For the person in the pew—by now Mass was celebrated in big

churches because of the vast number of Christians—the consecration became the high point of the liturgy. Emphasis fell not on receiving Jesus in Communion but on seeing and adoring the eucharistic Lord. This was so much the case that in 1215 the Fourth Lateran Council had to require by church law that Catholics receive Communion at least once a year. Practices that focused on eucharistic devotion sprang up: elevation of the host and chalice at Mass, benediction, exposition, Forty Hours and the feast of Corpus Christi (the Body of Christ).

Reformation to 20th Century. The 16th century brought about the Protestant Reformation. The Council of Trent (1545-1563) convened to correct some of the abuses which had crept into the church and also to defend some of the Catholic beliefs attacked by the Reformers. In the area of the Eucharist, the church Fathers defended the real presence of Jesus in the sacrament—body, blood, soul and divinity. They taught that the term "transubstantiation" correctly describes the total change that takes place in the words of consecration: the substance of the bread becomes Christ's body and the substance of the wine becomes his blood. They also stressed that the whole of the risen Jesus is present under each eucharistic form (bread and wine) and that to receive either the bread *or* the wine is to receive the whole Christ. Finally, against the attacks of the Reformers, the Fathers of the church reaffirmed that the Eucharist has the sacrificial character of Christ's sacrifice on the cross.

In the practice of the people, devotion to the Blessed Sacrament continued to flourish. People tended to receive Communion less frequently and often outside the context of the Mass. But in 1910, Pope Pius X extended an official invitation to the very young to receive Communion.

Today. As a result of the Second Vatican Council in the 1960s, the eucharistic celebration has been reformed. Chapters 1 and 2 of the Council's *Constitution on the Sacred Liturgy* gave a number of guidelines on how the Liturgy of Eucharist was to be updated. Among the changes that have made the Mass more meaningful to today's Catholics are the following:

1) The Mass is said in the language of the people so they can participate more fully in it.

2) The Prayer of the Faithful has been reintroduced.

3) On occasion we may receive the Eucharist under both species.

4) More emphasis is put on the Liturgy of the Word, with special guidelines to make the homily reflect the scripture readings.

5) Active participation of the laity—as servers, lectors, commentators, choir members—has been encouraged.

6) The practice of Communion in the hand is allowed. This latest change was adopted in the United States in 1977. It stresses that the Christian is consecrated in baptism and shares in the priesthood of Jesus Christ. Communion in the hand was the common practice in the first 1000 years of the church's history.

Today, the church is very concerned that people understand what is taking place at the Mass. The recent changes help us appreciate the Eucharist and participate in it more wholeheartedly. More than anything else, though, the post-Vatican II revisions emphasize the value of *communal* worship. They stress the importance of worshipping God as a community, united in a common bond of togetherness. Before these changes many Catholics tended to go to Mass and participate as passive observers, as individuals reciting their own prayers. Today, the emphasis is on community worship.

FOR ENRICHMENT

1. *Mass in the Early Church.* Read the following scripture passages. Then, in two paragraphs, briefly describe how the Mass was celebrated in the early church. Be sure to comment on St. Paul's criticism of the way in which some Corinthians were celebrating the Eucharist.

   Acts 2:42-46; 20:7-11; 27:35
   1 Cor 10:16-17; 11:17-34

2. Look up and report on the history of one of the following:

   benediction   Forty Hours devotion   novena
   devotion to the Sacred Heart of Jesus
   the feast of Corpus Christi

3. Interview your parents about the way in which Mass was celebrated before Vatican II. Draw up a list of changes which have been made since they were your age.

THE MEANING OF THE EUCHARIST TODAY

In a few short paragraphs, this section of the chapter will discuss what the Eucharist means to us who celebrate it today. Our participation in the Eucharist should be enriched if we understand more clearly what we are doing when we come together.

• *The Eucharist demonstrates God's continuous love for us.* Of all the sacraments, the Eucharist most dramatically symbolizes God's love affair with his people. Through the sacrament, the Son who accomplished salvation for us is given to us by the Father. What a tremendous gift and privilege—to be able to receive our Lord under the consecrated forms of bread and wine. The Eucharist is a continual reminder to us that God loves us, cares for us and comes to us in the most intimate way. He joins himself to us so that we may live his life of love. He becomes one with us so that we know in our hearts that we are united to our Lord and the source of our life. This great gift is ours for the taking. We need faith and we need to respond by accepting the gift.

• *The Mass remembers and re-enacts Christ's sacrifice on the cross.* The eucharistic celebration makes present and real the saving deeds that Jesus accomplished on the cross: the saving from sin and death. The effects of what he did once on the cross now touch us who commemorate his deeds today. The root meaning of *sacrifice* means "to make holy." The eucharistic sacrifice makes us holy, joins us to God the Father and frees us from the sin that keeps us separate from God and others.

• *The Eucharist creates and celebrates unity among Catholics.* Consider for a minute what happens when Catholics come to the

table of the Lord. All kinds of people—young and old, rich and poor, lovable and the unloved, saints and sinners—gather together and share the Lord among themselves. We eat of the same bread and drink of the same wine. Because we partake of the same Lord, we are united as one people, united more intimately than if we were blood brothers and sisters. The Eucharist is the prime symbol of our oneness. It both creates unity and is a celebration of that unity. Jesus makes us one and wants us to delight in our oneness. This is why the Eucharist is a real celebration—a joyous occasion. The Eucharist is the most powerful symbol of human unity because the principle of unity is God himself. Jesus' prayer for unity in John's Gospel (Jn 15:5) is accomplished in this sacrament.

• *The Mass reminds us of God's covenant of love and his command to love and serve others.* As indicated already, the Eucharist is a memorial meal of Jesus' new covenant of love. Jesus broke bread to symbolize the life he was to give up so that we could have eternal life; he poured wine to symbolize the salvation which is ours because he shed his blood. A covenant, though, demands response. The Eucharist reminds us that we are "to break ourselves," that is, to overcome our selfishness and serve others as Jesus served us. The Eucharist reminds us to "pour out our lives" for our fellow humans. At the end of the Mass, we are sent as Jesus was sent by the Father to share the good news. By breaking ourselves and pouring out our lives for others what we are really doing is loving. And the payoff to love is life—superabundant life. Jesus' resurrection proved this. We will experience the joys of his resurrection even in this life if we love as he did. We have his word on it:

> Jesus said, "I tell you solemnly, there is no one who has left house, brothers, sisters, father, children or land for my sake and for the sake of the gospel who will not be repaid a hundred times over, houses, brothers, sisters, mothers, children and land—not without persecutions—now in this present time and in the world to come, eternal life.
> "Many who are first will be last, and the last first" (Mk 10:29-31).

• *The Eucharist is the summit of Christian worship.* Because the church worships God the Father in Jesus Christ with the Holy Spirit, the Eucharist is a celebration of Christian life and identity formed by, in and through Jesus the Lord. The Eucharist is the highest form of worship for the Christian community. The community, gathered as one and united to the Risen Lord, offers its thanks and praise to the Creator for the marvelous deeds accomplished in Jesus. All the other sacraments are related to the Eucharist. Baptism incorporates us into the worshipping eucharistic community. Confirmation grants the fullness of the Spirit who moves us to worship the Father through Jesus in the Mass. The sacrament of reconciliation reunites us with the community of love which we have harmed by our sins so that we may worship with a pure heart. Christian marriage builds up the community of love while ordination singles out the Christian minister who stands between God and the community as the mediator of Christ in the Eucharist. The anointing of the sick prepares the sick for the heavenly eucharistic banquet—the ultimate feast for which Christians hope.

EXERCISES:

A. *What does the Eucharist mean to you?* Here are some Catholic beliefs about the Eucharist. Indicate your attitude on the continuum given. S.A.—strongly agree; N. O.—no opinion; S.D.—strongly disagree.

1. The Eucharist is a great action of love.

   S.A.   N.O.   S.D.

2. The Eucharist makes us holy.

   S.A.   N.O.   S.D.

3. The Eucharist is a symbol of unity with fellow Christians.

   S.A.   N.O.   S.D.

4. The Eucharist is a reminder to love others.

   S.A.   N.O.   S.D.

5. The best way to worship God is through the Eucharist.

   S.A.   N.O.   S.D.

Discuss:

1. Share your responses in class and give the reasons for your answers.

2. Did you disagree with any statement? Is there something you can do to make the Eucharist more meaningful and perhaps help you agree with the statement?

B. *Being present to others.*

1. What does it mean to be "present" to others? Indicate how you are present to someone in the following settings:

   a. through a letter

   b. being in the same room, but not paying attention to the person

   c. sharing a handshake or kiss

   d. giving a gift

2. *The Constitution on the Sacred Liturgy* teaches that Jesus is present in the liturgy in several ways. Explain what is meant by each kind of presence

   a. in the community gathered in Jesus' name

   b. in the hearts of individual Christians

   c. in the priest, Jesus' representative at Mass

   d. in the reading of Scripture

   e. in the consecrated bread and wine

3. *Reasons for going to Mass:* Which of the following reasons for going to Mass have you heard? Check off any that you think are immature reasons. What might you say to a person who gives one of these immature reasons for going? Could you convince him or her that there might be a better reason for participating?

   _____ If God has given me 168 hours in the week to live, I owe him at least an hour's worth of thanks.

   _____ Because I want to go to heaven.

   _____ If I don't, I'll go to hell.

   _____ It's church law and because I belong to the church I'd better follow the law.

   _____ To please my parents and keep peace at home.

   _____ God loves me and this is the best way to show him that I love him.

THE ORGANIZATION OF THE MASS

Much could be written about what takes place during the Mass. For our purposes, though, here is a very brief overview of the structure of the eucharistic liturgy with some comments on the significance of each of the actions. In conjunction with your study of this section of the chapter, please obtain a Sunday missalette and read the prayers for each section so that these brief comments will be more meaningful. Then do the exercise below to test your grasp of the various elements of the celebration.

	The actions of the Mass	Significance of the actions
Beginning of the Mass The Lord is present to those gathered in his name.	1. Entrance and entrance song	1. Calls the people into community and prepares for the celebration
	2. Kissing and bowing to the altar	2. A sign of respect and affection for Jesus, the true Lord and Priest of the community; a symbol of peace and love
	3. Penitential rite, "Lord have mercy"	3. As a community of sinners, the people beg God's forgiveness so that worship can take place with pure hearts
	4. Gloria (not always part of the Mass)	4. The community praises the Trinity
	5. Prayer of the day	5. Recalls the mystery of salvation proper to the day or feast

	The actions of the Mass	Significance of the actions
LITURGY OF THE WORD The Lord is present to the community in his word.	1. First reading and responsorial psalm	1. The Lord comes in his word
	2. Second reading, verse or Alleluia	2. With faith and reflection, the community receives God's word
	3. Gospel	3. The good news is heard (our link to the past)
	4. Homily	4. The proclaimer of the word relates it to everyday life (priest relates the good news to the present)
	5. Creed (not always part of Mass)	5. and 6. The community assents to the word by proclaiming its faith and asking for God's blessings and the salvation of the world (Community looks to *future*—its hopes)
	6. Intercession	
LITURGY OF THE EUCHARIST, Part 1 A memorial meal and a real sacrifice	*Preparing the gifts*	
	1. Procession with the gifts	1. A symbol of the community's willingness to give of itself
	2. Presentation of the gifts on the altar	2. These gifts are a symbol of God's gift, and are the result of human labor
	3. Private prayer of the priest; washing of the hands	3. Humility and purity are required for self-giving so that the gifts of bread and wine may become Christ's body and blood
	4. Prayer over the gifts— asking the Spirit to make holy	4. "Holy things to the holy"

	The actions of the Mass	Significance of the actions
LITURGY OF THE EUCHARIST, Part 2 Jesus Christ is sacramentally present in the form of bread and wine.	*Eucharistic prayer*	
	5. Dialogue with Preface and Holy, Holy, Holy	5. Praises God as Creator and Lord of history
	6. Invocation of the Spirit	6. Acknowledges the power of the Spirit
	7. Account of institution	7. Remembers and makes present Christ's sacrifice of his body and blood
	8. Remembering and prayer of offering	8. Christ takes the church into his once-for-all sacrifice
	9. Union with the Holy Spirit	9. Christ gives himself through the power of the Spirit in the sacred meal
	10. Intercessions	10. The community prays for the salvation of all, both living and dead
	11. Concluding doxology	11. Concludes thanksgiving with praise to the Trinity
	Communion	
	12. Our Father	12. Asks for daily bread and forgiveness
	13. Prayer for peace	13. Desires love and peace of Christ
	14. Breaking of the bread	14. Breaks one bread—symbol of unity—so all may share in same body
	15. Reception of Communion	15. Food of salvation. We become one in the Lord so that we can be one in loving others.
	16. Concluding prayer	16. Petitions the Lord that union with him will bear fruit in daily life
Conclusion	1. Final blessing	1. Blessing to celebrate our participation
	2. Dismissal	2. Go and live the Eucharist every day

EXERCISE:

1. Obtain a copy of a missalette used in your parish. Find the readings for one Sunday for this month. Read them. Then do the following:

   Summarize: (the good news of the *past* proclaimed.)

   Reading 1: _____

   _____

   Reading 2: _____

   Gospel: _____

   _____

Using these readings, make a short outline for two different homilies. Homily #1 is for your friends; homily #2 is for the group of Catholics you normally worship with. Make at least five points that will touch the lives of these various audiences. (Remember: A homily is different from a sermon. A homily *expands* or *elaborates* on the scripture readings.)

Homily *#1*	Homily *#2*

(The good news related to the *present* lives of the Christian Community.)

1._____	1._____
_____	_____
2._____	2._____
_____	_____
3._____	3._____
_____	_____
4._____	4._____
_____	_____
5._____	5._____
_____	_____

Deliver one of these homilies to the class. Have your classmates critique it.

2. What intercessory prayers would you offer at this Mass that would go along with your homily? List three of them.

(Christians look to the *future* in hope and anticipation.)

a. _____

b. _____

c. _____

3. Read one of the eucharistic prayers. Briefly explain its meaning. Write your own version of the prayer.

a. Explanation: _____

_____

_____

b. My version: _____

_____

_____

_____

_____

4. At the Presentation of the Gifts, bread and wine are offered to God. If you could substitute three things about you to offer, what would they be? For example, your mere presence at the Mass even though you don't wish to be there, a trying time this past week, etc.

1. _____

_____

2. _____

_____

3. _____

_____

5. If a non-Catholic friend came to Mass with you and asked what happens at Communion, what would you say?

_____

_____

_____

_____

_____

LIVING THE EUCHARIST

We come to Mass on Sunday with our fellow believers to worship God and thank him for what he has done for us. Sunday is the Lord's day; it is a little Easter commemorating Jesus' triumph over sin and death. By gathering together on this day, we respond to our friend Jesus' invitation to celebrate with our fellow Christians. It is a great privilege to accept that invitation and respond to it joyfully. We receive our Lord in order to become like him. The *passive* dimension of receiving spiritual food becomes *active* as we allow Jesus to take over our lives. We respond to him by actively living his love for others.

At times we may be tempted not to partake of the eucharistic celebration. Sometimes we are lazy. But laziness can be overcome if we remember all that the Lord has done for us. Sometimes we think we can worship God in nature or privately, but Jesus asks that we come to his Father in community to praise him and thank him. At other times we lament the apparent hypocrisy of those attending Mass. But we should never forget that Jesus came precisely to associate with and save sinners and that we too are often hypocritical—we fail to live up to the ideals we profess. At still other times we don't feel that we get that much out of the Mass. But perhaps the reason is that we fail to put much *into* the Mass. We receive to the degree that we give. We go not to be entertained but to worship and praise God. The gift we get in return is Jesus himself.

What a loving thing to celebrate the Eucharist even when we don't feel like it. By attending the liturgy we are telling the Christian community that we care about it and that we deeply want to be part of it. To follow Jesus means to follow him with others. Our religion is not a private thing but a social thing of sharing and loving.

We live the Eucharist by joyfully attending it, receiving the Lord and then taking him into the world of school, work and home. We live the Lord's life by caring as he cared, by understanding as he understood, by loving as he loved. Our Catholic faith will be believable to others in the world today *only* to the degree that we allow the Jesus we receive at the Eucharist to shine through us to all those we meet. What an honor—what a responsibility—to be Christ for others. This is the challenge and the privilege of this important sacrament, the Eucharist.

EXERCISE:

List three ways you can live the Eucharist in your own life:

a. _____

_____

b. _____

_____

c. _____

_____

SUMMARY

1. *Eucharist* means "thanksgiving." Another popular term for the Eucharist is "Mass" which emphasizes our commission to live a Christlike life.

2. Our Eucharist is based on the Last Supper, a Passover Meal in which Jesus invested new meaning. He created a new covenant in his blood and gave us his own life under the forms of bread and wine.

3. Certain elements of the Mass have developed over the ages. Today, active participation of the laity is stressed very much.

4. The theology of the Eucharist stresses that the Eucharist:

- demonstrates God's love for us
- re-enacts Christ's sacrifice on the cross
- creates and celebrates Catholic unity

- reminds us of God's covenant of love and our responsibility to love and serve others
- is the summit of Christian worship

5. Each part of the Mass—and expecially the Liturgy of the Word and the Liturgy of the Eucharist—is filled with significance.

6. We live the Eucharist by allowing the Jesus we receive at Communion to shine forth in our daily lives.

EVALUATION

To test your understanding of this chapter, here are 10 statements about the Mass. In your notebook briefly (no more than three sentences) explain what each one means.

1. "Go, you are sent."

2. The Eucharist is a sacrifice.

3. Jesus is present at the liturgy under the forms of bread and wine.

4. The Eucharist is a celebration.

5. Communion means being with another person for that other person's sake.

6. The Eucharist is a memorial meal.

7. It is a privilege to go to Mass.

8. The Eucharist is a sacrament.

9. The Eucharist means love.

10. The Eucharist creates and celebrates unity.

ADDITIONAL EXERCISE

A fine way to conclude this chapter is to celebrate the Eucharist with your classmates. The church allows a certain amount of creativity, variety and spontaneity in the liturgy. Planning, though, is essential. Use the following checklist to plan your own liturgy. Perhaps you can use some of the prayers and homilies you and your classmates composed for this unit.

Theme: (for example—friendship with the Lord, unity, Spirit):

_____

where: _____   when: _____

celebrant: _____   vestments: _____

banners/posters: _____   made by: _____

other decorations: (e.g. flowers) _____

bread: _____

Songs: entrance: _____

Response after reading: _____

Presentation of the Gifts: _____

Acclamation: _____

Communion: _____

closing: _____

Readings: commentator: _____

1st reading: _____ read by: _____

2nd reading: _____ read by: _____

Response: _____ read by: _____

Gospel: _____ read by: _____

homilist: _____

Petitions: 1) _____ by: _____

2) _____ by: _____

3) _____ by: _____

4) _____ by: _____

5) _____ by: _____

Gifts: Presented by:

a. _____   a. _____

b. _____   b. _____

c. _____   c. _____

d. _____   d. _____

Eucharistic Prayer: _____

Other things:

Slide show: _____

Drama or dance: _____

Procession: _____

Mass servers: _____

_____

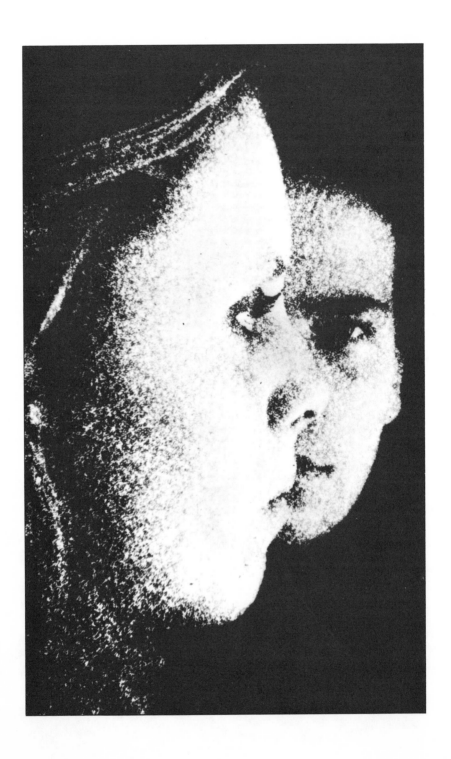

6

Forgiveness—
The Sacrament of
Reconciliation

In the evening of that same day, the first day of the week, the doors were closed in the room where the disciples were, for fear of the Jews. Jesus came and stood among them. He said to them, "Peace be with you," and showed them his hands and his side. The disciples were filled with joy when they saw the Lord, and he said to them again, "Peace be with you."

"As the Father sent me,
so am I sending you."

After saying this he breathed on them and said:

"Receive the Holy Spirit.
For those whose sins you forgive,
they are forgiven;
for those whose sins you retain,
they are retained."

—Jn 20:19-23

It is most revealing in John's Gospel that when Jesus first appeared to the apostles on Easter Sunday he gave them the power to forgive sins in his name. Carefully read the opening passage again. In it, Jesus commissions his followers to do the same kind of thing he was sent to do: forgive sins. What a tremendous gift this is—to be freed from the evil of sin.

This power of forgiving sins is most fully expressed and

157

celebrated in the sacrament of reconciliation, a sacrament of spiritual healing. Along with the anointing of the sick (see Chapter 7), this sacrament extends the Lord's healing and forgiving touch into the world today. What a tremendous privilege to encounter the Divine Physician, our loving brother in these two sacraments!

Jesus is our Savior. He has come to free us from our sins. When we recognize that we are weak, when we fall short of our goals, when we fail to love God through others, we can turn to him who saves us from sinful habits. By appreciating how sinful we can be at times, we will tend to turn more and more to our friend and Savior, Jesus Christ, who is always there to help us and lead us to his Father.

This chapter will look at the sacrament of reconciliation by first discussing the reality of sin. Then, we shall look at how Jesus related to sinners in his earthly ministry. This will be followed by a brief look at the history of the sacrament and its meaning for us today. Finally, the current rite of reconciliation will be outlined with some discussion on the role this sacrament can play in the life of a young Christian. Let's begin, though, with the following exercises.

GETTING STARTED

A. *AN INVENTORY ON THE SACRAMENT OF RECONCILIATION.* What are your attitudes to this sacrament? Please complete the following sentences and then discuss your remarks with your classmates. Are your answers similar? Why or why not?

1. I go to confession when _____

2. My description of a good confessor is _____

_____

3. My best experience with this sacrament was _____

_____

4. My worst experience with this sacrament was _____

_____

5. The most meaningful penance given to me was _____

_____

6. What I like least about this sacrament is _____

_____

7. This sacrament would mean more to me if _____

_____

B. *MY APPROACH TO MORALITY.* Here are some statements about morality, that is, the rightness or wrongness of human actions.
Answer "true" or "false" to the following statements. Then, decide if your answer is Christian or not.

True/False

_____ 1. Something is all right if the majority thinks it is all right.

_____ 2. It is OK to drink alcoholic beverages before driving as long as no one gets hurt.

_____ 3. I have the duty to give to the poor even if I have to deny myself some fun times.

_____ 4. It is OK for me to take supplies from an office if I don't take much.

_____ 5. People should be allowed to exclude anyone they want from their neighborhood.

_____ 6. I always have the duty to follow my conscience.

_____ 7. Americans should not feel unduly concerned about having so much material wealth. They should thank God for his blessings and not worry too much about giving a lot of their wealth away.

_____ 8. We must be just to people, that is, give them their due. But we don't have to be charitable, that is, give them more than their due.

_____ 9. In quite a few cases known to me, premarital sexual activity is OK.

_____ 10. I have to love others but I don't have to like them.

Discuss: a. Share your responses.
b. What makes something Christian or unchristian?

C. *WHAT IS SIN?* Here are several definitions of sin. Rank them from (1) the best definition to (9) the least helpful definition. Discuss.

____ Sin is a breaking of God's law

____ Sin is a breaking of church law

____ Sin is going against one's conscience

____ Sin is the breaking of relationships

____ Sin is a lack of love

____ Sin is being coldhearted and stiff-necked

____ Sin is a refusal to grow

____ Sin is being more concerned with self than with others

____ Sin makes God and others objects rather than persons

____ Sin is the breaking of human laws and rules

WHAT IS SIN?

Has anyone recently stolen something from you? Cheated you? Cursed you? What is your reaction when you read the newspaper? Do the number of abortions, deaths from starvation (about 10,000 people per day), terrorist actions, threats of war and actual combat—do these things and countless others like them bother you? And what about yourself? How do you feel when you fall back into the same nasty habits after resolving not to do so—habits like cheating, lying, drinking, giving in to sexual temptation and the like? When you react to these things, you are reacting to sin. Sin is all over the place—it is in the world and it is in our own lives. Many years ago St. Paul wrote: "I cannot understand my own behaviour. I fail to carry out the things I want to do, and I find myself doing the very things I hate . . . instead of doing the good things I want to do, I carry out the sinful things I do not want" (Rom 7:15,19).

Some Biblical Reflections on Sin. Sin is called "missing the mark" in the Scriptures. Missing the mark meant failing to conform to God's covenant of love. By not loving, which is what God expects of his children, we sin. The Bible also calls sin "hardness of heart." This image is based on the heart as the symbol of love and stresses, once again, that sin is a failure to love. Sin is a failure to love God above all things and our neighbor as ourselves. The Old Testament calls sinners "foolish people" (Dt 32:6). It is indeed foolish not to respond to a loving God with love.

Some more precision. Sin is attitude and action. Sin is a failure to act. Finally, sin is a power.

1. Sin as attitude. What God requires of us is an open, loving heart which responds to him through worship and praise and loves him through others. But sometimes we freeze our hearts against God. We make ourselves the number one person in our lives. We, in effect, worship ourselves and fail to consider the source of our life and our many gifts. This reality often takes on an attitude of pride, an attitude that we can go it alone without God or without others. Because of this attitude, or others like it—sloth, envy and the like—we can become insensitive to others.

2. Sin as action and as failure to act. This insensitivity can lead us to do harmful things against God and neighbor. For example, because we're more concerned about ourselves than about others, we may be inclined to steal or misuse our gift of sexuality to get pleasure just for ourselves. These acts flow from the attitude of a cold heart before God and others. But sinful self-sufficiency can also lead to not doing for others—failure to act when we should. For example, because we are so self-centered, we can neglect to give to the poor or we can turn away from a situation that calls for positive action. This certainly was the sin of the Levite and priest in the parable of the Good Samaritan (Lk 10:25-37). Sin can be, then, action or failure to act.

3. Sin as power. Lastly, sin can be an all-pervasive power which seems to have a life of its own. For example, sin can be imbedded in institutions. Governments, for instance, can have long-standing policies of discrimination against certain groups. These policies are so powerful that it is very difficult for one person or even a group of people to break that power. War, terrorism, exploitation by large corporations are all examples of the power of sin which is strongly at work in the world.

Our tendency to sin, to turn away from God, neighbor and self also illustrates the power of sin in the world. Traditional Catholic theology holds that this kind of power is the result of original sin. And St. Paul reminds us that by our own efforts we cannot overcome this power, this condition. However, we believe that Jesus can conquer and has defeated sin and its effects. It is up to us to allow Jesus into our lives and into the world so that his love can warm our frozen hearts and defeat the power of sin in our lives and in the world.

The effects of sin. Sin alienates us from God, from neighbor and from self. By saying no to God's invitation to love through Jesus, we have separated ourselves from God. This separation causes us to hate ourselves and to be distant from others. For example, when we lie, we refuse to love the truth. Remember, Jesus said that he is the truth. By lying, we turn away from the source of our life. This turning away causes us to be false people. We are not true to ourselves and have created a kind of split in ourselves. We thus separate ourselves from what is true in us when we lie. And because we have deceived another person, we have separated ourselves from others as well. We are no longer trustworthy; people don't know if they can believe us or not. We have alienated ourselves.

All sin has social consequences, too. What we do or don't do, the attitudes we have or don't have affect others. This is true because we are social beings, with and for others. For example, if I have a prejudiced attitude, this will affect my dealings with everyone. Even if I don't say something prejudiced or commit some violent act harmful to another, my prejudiced personality—my sinful attitude—will show up in all my dealings with others. My prejudice will make me more narrow-minded and less able to relate openly with others. And all who have dealings with me will be affected by this sinful attitude of mine. You can analyze any sin this way—it always affects others. As we shall see, this is why the sacrament of reconciliation today stresses the need to make things right (that is, reconcile) with the community whom we have harmed with our sin. This sacrament is a powerful sign of healing the wounds we have created in our relationships with God, self and others.

Degrees of sin. Catholic theology has distinguished degrees of sinfulness. Here are the common degrees:

a. Mortal sin. This is an attitude, action or failure to act that destroys our relationship with God and others. It is very serious. In mortal sin we are in effect saying, "I don't want God's love; I merely want myself." It is not easy for a person who is generally loving to turn so abruptly from the source of his or her love, but it is possible. It is possible to murder, to commit adultery, to deny God, to cruelly break up a marriage, to neglect the poor and sick and old. Because God always loves us, though, the warmth of his love can bring back to life even the sinner who has chosen to close his or her heart to God and neighbor. Mortal sin is forgiven and life restored whenever the sinner remembers God's incredible love, turns away from the life of sin and accepts the Father's ever-present offer to love.

To commit deadly sin, though, three conditions are necessary:

(1) *What I do must be seriously wrong.* It must of itself kill a love relationship. (It is easy to see, for example, how murder kills a relationship or how neglect of the starving poor in our midst is seriously wrong.)

(2) *I must know that what I do is seriously wrong.* We are not morally blameworthy for what we don't know is wrong. But we have a serious obligation to find out the truth, too. A closed mind in itself is a grave wrong. The person following Christ must have an open mind to learning the truth, especially in matters that affect our relationship with God and neighbor.

(3) *I must choose to do the wrong.* Freedom of choice is

necessary for doing serious harm to our love relationship with God and neighbor. Certain things like passion, force and fear tend to destroy our freedom and can cause us to do something we would not ordinarily do or fail to do something we ordinarily would do. We have an obligation, though, to avoid those occasions and situations where we know our freedom will be lessened.

b. Venial sin. Venial sin is an offense against God or neighbor which does not kill the relationship. It is a stumbling, as it were, on the path of following Jesus our Lord. For example, a sarcastic remark or the theft of a very small amount of money normally does not kill our relationship with another. But venial sin is not something we should treat lightly, because it is still a failure to grow. Friends are concerned about the quality of their relationship. The friend of Jesus, too, should want to uproot any attitude or problem that crops up in the relationship.

c. Serious sin. Today, some Catholic theologians write about a third kind of sin—serious sin. Something was done or not done that has a tendency to break off love relationships. To an outside observer it may look as though we have destroyed a relationship. But perhaps full consent of the will was not given. The act or attitude does not represent a clear turning away from our basic commitment to God and others. Nevertheless, the foundation of the relationship has been shaken seriously. A pattern of this kind of sin may very well lead—and shortly—to the death blow for our love of God and neighbor.

We Christians are concerned about sin in our lives. We want to be close to God and neighbor. We both want and need our Lord's forgiving touch—a touch that warms our hearts to his love and a touch that brings back to life dead relationships and heals the scars of wounded lives. The good news of the sacrament of reconciliation is that we have a clear sign of this forgiving, healing touch of our Lord. It is a great opportunity for us to hear the good news of Jesus and be reconciled to him and to our neighbor. Certainly the Christian who wants to use every opportunity to grow closer in love and be reconciled to those he or she has harmed will use this sacramental sign to its full advantage.

SOME EXERCISES ON SIN

1. Make a list of actions that you see among people your age which can kill a love relationship. Why are they so serious?

action	*reason*
_____	_____
_____	_____
_____	_____

Make a list of ways in which *not* acting can also kill a love relationship.

failure to act	*reason*
_____	_____
_____	_____
_____	_____

What are some actions that, while they don't kill a relationship, prevent it from growing? Some failures to act? Why do you see these things as less serious than the ones above?

_____	_____
_____	_____
_____	_____

2. Discuss the following situations. Are they serious enough to destroy a relationship? Could they be done without full knowledge? full consent? If they are not serious enough to destroy the relationship, in what ways do they damage it? Are they wrong at all?

   a. A woman becomes pregnant through artificial insemination with sperm from an anonymous donor. Her husband approves of the procedure.

   b. A woman has a five-week-old embryo aborted.

   c. A clinic dispenses contraceptive pills to high school students, without the need for parental permission.

   d. A group engages in a defamation campaign to remove a black legislator from office.

   e. The "jocks" in a class refuse to associate with others not in their group.

   f. A friend sells drugs to her classmates.

   g. A student regularly copies homework from a friend because he has a job.

3. Here are some *attitudes*. Place a check mark (✓) to the left of those that seem to describe you. Place an *X* to the right of any that you wish you could get rid of.

__ lazy__	__ selfish__	__ truthful__
__ thoughtful__	__ cynical__	__ honest__
__ prideful__	__ skeptical__	__ resentful__
__ closed-minded__	__ trusting__	__ joyous__
	__ jealous__	__ sad__
__ optimistic__	__ open-minded__	__ lustful__
__ greedy__		

Now, list three attitudes from those above which can cause problems in a relationship. Name something that flows from these attitudes which a person could do or might fail to do that would be sinful.

_____

_____

_____

_____

JESUS AND SINNERS

Our Lord's entire earthly ministry was a mission of mercy for sinners. As we saw in the words of institution for the Eucharist, Jesus died for the sins of people. He is God the Father's incredible gift of love, God's living sign of forgiveness to us sinners.

Jesus came for sinners. He associated with them, loved them and forgave them. This association brought him much criticism. You might recall from Matthew's Gospel the time he was criticized for being with the hated tax collectors and other outcasts (Mt 9:9-13). The general belief among the Pharisees and other Jewish leaders of our Lord's day was that a person associating with sinners would be contaminated by that association. But remember Jesus' answer to them:

"It is not the healthy who need the doctor, but the sick. Go and learn the meaning of the words: 'What I want is mercy, not sacrifice.' And indeed I did not come to call the virtuous, but sinners" (Mt 9:12-13).

Jesus loved sinners. He forgave the condemned criminal on

the cross next to him and promised him paradise (Lk 23:32-43). He loved the woman caught in adultery, saving her life when she was threatened with death by stoning. But he also told her to avoid sin in the future (Jn 8:1-11). He praised the faith of the woman who approached him while he was dining in the house of the Pharisee Simon and he forgave her many sins (Lk 7:36-50). He lovingly forgave his persecutors while he hung on the cross, despite their taunts and their jeers (Lk 23:34).

His teaching about his Father had at its heart a message of forgiving love. Perhaps the greatest story in the world is the parable of the Prodigal Son (Lk 15:11-32). The father in the story extended his heartfelt love to the son who squandered his every possession and who committed every sin in the book. The son was so desperate that he ate with the pigs who scrounged for fodder from the field. Recalling the goodness of his father, the son returned home. The father did not make the son beg for forgiveness, but rather ran out to embrace him and joyfully celebrate his return. The father even lovingly forgave (and did not criticize) the older brother for his carping jealousy. The father in the parable is like our Lord and God—loving and forgiving, ever anxious for our return.

We should never forget these examples from Jesus' teaching and life. He came precisely to save sinners. He reminds us that his Father will always forgive us, that his love is always there. We need but turn to him and accept the great gift that is ours. This is the essence of the good news of Jesus: He loves us, he stands ready *always* to forgive us. We should never, never forget this good news in a world which reports only bad news. God is love; God is forgiveness. This is the message and life of Jesus Christ.

SOME WRITTEN REFLECTIONS

1. *A Meditation.* Surely you have heard the expression, "Christ came to save mankind." Translate this, though, into: "Jesus came to save *me.*" Imagine Jesus hanging on the cross and you standing nearby. His eyes meet yours. Miraculously, he comes down from the cross and embraces you. Picture this scene and then write in your journal what you would think and feel.

    a. What would he say to you? What would you say to him?

    b. What do you feel as he dies—in your arms?

    c. Can you feel the resurrected life and the love of his Father flow through him to you? Describe it.

2. Write your own version of the Prodigal Son, Lk 15:11-32. Write it as a modern play and perhaps have a few classmates act it out with you for the penance service at the end of this chapter.

3. Read the Zacchaeus story in Lk 19:1-10. Write a short interpretation of it.

4. Write an essay about a time when you either forgave or were forgiven. Report your reactions to the experience, especially your feelings. Witness to your faith by sharing this essay with one other person.

THE SACRAMENT OF RECONCILIATION THROUGH THE AGES

The history of the sacrament of reconciliation is long and complex. This section presents a very simplified overview of how this sacrament developed into what we have today.

New Testament times. The story of this sacrament begins, of course, with the ministry and message of Jesus. This story, as we have just seen, is a message of God's incredible love and forgiveness of sinners. In the New Testament, baptism is the primary way that the power of sin is overcome in the life of the believer. A question soon arose, though: What would happen to a person who sinned against God and the community after baptism? As we saw in John's Gospel, Jesus certainly gave the power to bind or loose sin to the apostles (see also Mt 16:19 and 18:18).

In evidence in the epistles are some hints of this power being used. St. Paul referred to what should be done to a Christian who refused to live up to the Christian call. The danger with such a sinner was that he provided bad example to the Christian community. Paul says, for example, that Christians should show the love of Christ to sinners (2 Cor 2:5-11), expecially to sinners who repent of their sins. Paul reminds his fellow believers that a sinner is to be admonished several times and, if the sinner still does not repent, he or she should be excluded from the community (2 Thes 3:14 and 1 Cor 5:1-5).

Early church (second to fifth centuries) Public Penance. A major concern in the early church was how to deal with mortal sin. Venial sin was more easily handled: It was forgiven through participation in the Eucharist, through prayer and by works of mercy like almsgiving. But how was mortal sin dealt with? Mortal sin was a deep-rooted problem that required much work on the part of the sinner before he or she could change and return fully to the community. In this period, the belief was that mortal sin could be forgiven, but usually just once in a person's lifetime.

The practice of penance in this period seems harsh by modern standards. The sinner entered into an order called Penitents, confessed his or her sin to the bishop and then had to do public penance for a period often lasting years. Reconciliation was a long process involving the need for the penitent to be sponsored again by a fellow Christian. The public sins which required this kind of process included apostasy (denying Christ), adultery and murder. Penances included not only wearing sackcloth and ashes but refraining from marital relations, fasting and abstaining from meat.

Because of the severity of the penances given in the early centuries to those entering the Order of Penitents, people often delayed reception of the sacrament until they were close to death. The sacrament was considered a "second baptism" and people did not take it lightly. The doing of penance was of major importance in the process of reconciliation. It clearly demonstrated to the community harmed by the sin that the sinner indeed repented.

Early Middle Ages (sixth to 12th centuries) Private Confession. The harshness of the practice of the early church inevitably brought a change in this sacrament. More and more often people avoided receiving the sacrament until the end of their lives and as a result stayed away from the eucharistic table. Around the sixth century the Irish monks began the practice of private confession. The monks in the monastery would select a spiritual director who would hear their confessions of sin and absolve them. This practice caught on with the lay people around the monasteries and eventually spread throughout Europe.

The chart below shows some of the differences between the approach of the early church and that of the early Middle Ages in the practice of this sacrament. However, it should be pointed out that the practice of public penance continued through this later period, too.

Early Church: Public Penance	*Middle Ages: Private Confession*
1. Only certain very serious sins were confessed—often only once in a lifetime.	1. All sins could be confessed—as often as desired.
2. Confession to a bishop, and public penance.	2. Confession to a priest in private.
3. A long period of satisfaction before reconciliation with the community.	3. Penance given from a book and then performed by the penitent.
4. A solemn reconciliation ceremony in Holy Week—a "second baptism."	4. Penitent returned for final absolution. (Major Development: around A.D. 1000 absolution was given right after confession.)

Later Middle Ages (12th through 15th centuries) Theology of the Sacrament. During this period, theologians gave precision to the practice of the sacrament. For example, in 1215 the Fourth Lateran Council taught that all Catholics must confess all serious sins to their pastor at least once a year. Stress was put on absolution. Around this time, too, theologians wrote that confession of sins to lay persons—a practice in the church from the earliest times—did not constitute a sacrament.

St. Thomas Aquinas defined the nature of the sacrament very carefully. He said that the entire sacrament is both the sign of and the cause of the sinner's forgiveness. It is God's grace that gives love to the sinner to turn his or her heart to the sacrament. Contrition—true sorrow for sin—wipes out the sin. Sacramental confession is necessary for the forgiveness of mortal sin. Both the penance and the absolution together form the sacrament.

Sixteenth century to Modern Times. The Role of the Council of Trent. As we saw in the last chapter, the Council of Trent had to answer some of the objections of the Reformers concerning sacramental practice. The Council's teachings did draw some clear distinctions to defend the Catholic practice of reconciliation. These distinctions might sound legalistic but they certainly were necessary to defend the sacrament. Here are some of them:

a. Penance is truly a sacrament.

b. "Perfect contrition" is motivated by true love of God. It does forgive sin. It includes a desire to receive the sacrament in the future.

c. "Imperfect contrition" is motivated by the seriousness, number and disgracefulness of sin and the realization that heaven is lost and eternal damnation incurred. It does not forgive sin by itself but disposes a person to receive the sacrament.

d. When confessing mortal sin, the penitent should mention the kind of sin committed and the number of times.

e. Confession of sin is of divine institution.

f. Bishops and priests have the power to forgive sin. They have a serious obligation to impose a penance because there are remnants of sin (temporal punishment due to sin) even after receiving the sacrament.

This period also saw the introduction of the screen between the priest and the penitent to protect the anonymity of the sinner. Confessions were to be done in church in a confessional. These requirements brought a certain solemnity to the sacrament and made it a more worshipful experience.

When parishes remained small, the sacrament was also used to get personal spiritual counseling from the priest. With the growth of large parishes, though, this practice of personal counseling became very difficult to carry out.

Reconciliation Today. The name of the sacrament through the ages is quite revealing. In the early years, *penance* seemed to be the focus. Harsh, long penances were assigned for the sinner to root out the sin in his or her life. Later on, *confession* in private, with a priest judging so that he could give absolution, became the practice. For many people the confession itself became more difficult than the penance assigned. Today, the focus of the sacrament is on neither penance nor confession as such. Rather, the sacrament of *reconciliation* today stresses the need for the sinner to be healed of sin so that true reconciliation can take place with God and neighbor.

In the reform of the sacrament (1974), the stress has been on making the sacrament a real sign of healing. There is space in the new liturgy of reconciliation for the declaration of God's healing word. Confession rooms have been introduced to create a feeling of warmth and welcome and are especially helpful if a person wishes to confess face-to-face. Throughout, the priest is to create a friendly, encouraging, prayerful atmosphere so that the sinner experiences the healing touch of Jesus Christ who makes him or her whole again, reconciled with God and the Christian community. Provision is even made today for *communal* celebrations of this reconciling peace of Jesus (with the individual confession of sins) to underscore the need to be reunited in love with *both* God and the community.

SOME EXERCISES

1. *Penances.* As a class, make up your own *Penitential Book.* What do you think would be a good penance, both meaningful and helpful, to give for each of these common sins?

Sin	*Penance*
disrespect of a parent	_____
	_____
habitual cheating at studies	_____
	_____
abuse of the body through alcohol or drugs	_____
	_____
failure to pray	_____
	_____
neglect of the poor	_____
prejudiced behavior	_____
	_____
misuse of sexual powers and gifts	_____
	_____
swearing	_____
	_____
giving bad example to a younger person	_____
	_____

2. *Research* how the practice of reconciliation takes place in another Christian denomination or in the Jewish community. Make a report to the class.

3. *Discuss:* What would you say to people who make these two statements?

> a. "I don't know why I have to confess to a priest."
>
> b. "I'm afraid to go to confession."

4. *Mature vs. Immature.* Here are some questions a person might ask in an examination of conscience before making a

confession. Do you think they are questions a mature Christian or an immature Christian would ask? Mark *M* for mature; *I* for immature.

_____ How have I helped the old people in my community?

_____ How far can I go in sexual matters before committing a serious sin?

_____ How long must my prayers be to have any value?

_____ How much respect do I owe my teachers?

_____ How can I help a lonely classmate?

_____ How can I best prepare for my future life?

_____ If I earn a lot of money, how much must I give to charities?

_____ Can I cheat without sinning?

_____ If I forgive a person once, do I have to forgive him or her again for doing the same thing to me?

Discuss your responses and give reasons for them.

PROCESS OF RECONCILIATION

The humble and sincere Catholic realizes that sin is all over his or her life. This is not startling; it is part of the human condition. But the follower of Jesus should be disturbed at this reality, disturbed to the point of doing something about it. Catholics are privileged to have a concrete sign of Christ's forgiveness in the sacrament of reconciliation. It is a tremendous sign of Jesus' friendship and a valuable opportunity to help uproot sin that keeps us from getting even closer to the Lord.

Let us briefly look at the four parts of the sacrament treated in the revised rite of the sacrament of reconciliation.

1. Contrition. The most important action of the penitent is to approach the sacrament with a contrite heart. *Contrition* is defined as "heartful sorrow and aversion for the sin committed along with the intention of sinning no more." God's love moves us to sorrow. The biblical term for this is *metanoia,* a change of heart whereby we model our lives on Jesus. If we have true sorrow for our sins, we are surely going to derive great benefit from the sacrament. We will tend to have a warm heart that beats with the love of God. Contrition, then, is a necessary step in approaching the sacrament.

2. Confession. The Holy Spirit moves us to have a sorrowful heart and it is his prompting that leads us to the Lord in this sacrament. Confession of sin to the priest is an *external* sign that our *internal* sorrow is genuine. Confession assures our sincerity, makes us openly humble before the Lord and demonstrates faith in our Lord's saving touch.

Confession of sin can be difficult for us sometimes. No one denies this. However, confession of sin is a strong sign of our trust in the Lord and a convincing symbol to us that we sincerely have sorrow for our sins. In facing up to our sin we, in fact, take it to the Lord for his healing touch. To speak the sin is to face up to it and to mean the expression of sorrow behind it. In fact, psychologists claim that verbally expressing our deeply hidden problems and inclinations is essential to the healing process. So, too, in the sacrament of reconciliation. Examining our inner heart and externally accusing ourselves should, furthermore, *always* be made in light of God's loving mercy. We confess because we know that he loves us and wants us to face up to the truth about ourselves. The priest can help us when we confess our sins, too. Through spiritual counselling and encouragement he can embody our Lord's words of forgiveness, concern and love.

3. Act of penance (satisfaction). True conversion leads to acts of penance or satisfaction for the sins committed: turning away from our former way of conduct and repairing any harm done. The penances assigned by the priest should fit the penitent, the harm done and the spiritual sickness that needs curing. We should not view these acts of penance as burdens. Rather, we should be grateful to God that we have an opportunity to help repair any damage our sins did. We should also thank God for the opportunity they afford us to be compassionate and generously involved. By performing them—prayers, good works, etc.—we help put the sin behind us so that we can once again get on the road of following the Lord.

4. Absolution. The words of absolution recited by the priest are the prayer of the church to God for the sinner. The words are a visible sign of the Father's loving forgiveness. They reassure the contrite penitent that God's forgiveness has definitely been given. They are joyful, faith-filled words of Christ's love for us.

As we saw in our discussion of the Council of Trent, Catholics are obligated to confess by number and kind every mortal sin they remember committing. However, we are encouraged by the church to receive this sacrament as a helpful remedy for lesser sins. The sacrament is a powerful reminder to all sinners—grave and less serious—that our goal as individuals and as a community is to conform ourselves to Christ. The true test of whether this conformity takes place is whether we grow in service to both God and neighbor.

AN EXAMINATION OF CONSCIENCE

Where can you grow in love of God, neighbor and self? Are your actions, choices and attitudes loving, moral ones? Do they:

- stand up to the glare of publicity?
- build up your trust and honesty with others?
- tend to unite you with others?
- give you a sense of personal integrity (proud of what you have done, what you believe, how you act)?
- make you more generally loving, looking at the best in people?
- bring you a genuine feeling of peace, of knowing you did the right thing, of joyfulness?

If you answer "Yes" to these questions and questions like them, you are doing well. But can you grow? Here is an examination of conscience based on the categories of love of God, self and neighbor. Single out one area in each category where you feel you need our Lord's special help. Take these "areas that need growth" to our Lord in the sacrament of reconciliation.

I. Love God above All Things

Do I pray each day? Do I think of God and thank him often for all he has done for me?

Do I participate in Mass or do I attend grudgingly?

Is the Father my friend? Do I spend time with him? With our Lord Jesus? Do I ask for the strength of the Spirit?

Do I see our Lord in others?

Am I respectful of God in my language? How about with Jesus' mother, our mother Mary?

Do I trust our Lord when things are going poorly?

Do I try to learn more about my religion at school? in parish programs? through reading?

II. Love Neighbor

Do I love others as much as myself? My family, my friends, my classmates, others I meet each day?

Do I respect my parents, my teachers, other authority figures?

Do I help my parents with expenses as best as I can?

Do I try to be the center of attention or do I go out of my way to involve others in conversation?

Am I jealous? possessive of my goods? selfish with my time?

Am I honest when talking about others? Do I cheat on tests? Do I steal?

Do I make fun of others who are different? other races? those who disagree with me? those who don't hang around with me?

Have I done anything for the poor, the sick, the lonely, the old (perhaps my grandparents)?

Do I try to befriend others, especially those whom I may not particularly like?

Do I use other people? Do I use their bodies for my sexual gratification? Do I see them as my brother or sister, as an image of God?

Do I empathize with others, especially the suffering?

Do I build myself up while I tear others down? Do I spread gossip? Do I accept differences of opinion? Can I keep confidences?

Am I obedient? Do I drive carefully and respect the property of others?

III. Love Self

Do I thank God for making me the way I am or do I belittle my particular talents and gifts?

Do I mistreat my body with drugs and alcohol? Do I get enough rest and recreation?

Do I study?

Do I stand on my own two feet or do I let others make decisions for me?

Do I use my sexual powers lovingly and respectfully? Am I modest?

Do I look to others for help or do I try to "go it alone"?

Am I a good friend?

Do I waste money on frivolous things? Do I share it with others?

Do I appreciate what I have?

THE RITE OF RECONCILIATION FOR ONE PENITENT

(The general format for the communal rite of reconciliation will be presented in the penance service at the end of this chapter.)

1. The priest welcomes the penitent.

2. The penitent (sometimes with the priest) begins with the Sign of the Cross.

3. The priest warmly encourages the penitent to trust God. He has a choice of texts to which the penitent answers "Amen."

4. *Reading the Word of God* (optional). The theme of the reading is God's mercy and the call to conversion. Here are some sample readings: Mt 6:14-15; Mk 1:14-15; Lk 15:1-7; Lk 6:31-38; Rom 5:8-9; Col 3:8-10 and 12-17; 1 Jn 1:6-7 and 9.

5. *Confession of sin.* If it is customary, the penitent can use a general formula for confession of sin. If necessary, the priest can help the penitent make a good confession and can help with suitable counsel. He encourages the penitent to true sorrow and brings to mind the need for the penitent to join in our Lord's death and resurrection. The priest assigns a penance which he judges will help the sinner.

6. *Act of Contrition.* The priest now asks the penitent to express externally the sorrow which is already present in the penitent's heart. This act of contrition can be expressed in any way or can be the traditional one given here:

   > My God,
   > I am sorry for my sins with all my heart.
   > In choosing to do wrong
   > and failing to do good,
   > I have sinned against you
   > whom I should love above all things.
   > I firmly intend, with your help,
   > to do penance,
   > to sin no more,
   > and to avoid whatever leads me to sin.
   > Our Savior Jesus Christ
   > suffered and died for us.
   > In his name, my God, have mercy.

7. *Absolution.* The words of absolution emphasize the action of the Trinity:

> (The priest extends his hands over the penitent's head or extends his right hand):

> God, the Father of mercies,
> through the death and resurrection of his Son
> has reconciled the world to himself
> and sent the Holy Spirit among us
> for the forgiveness of sins;
> through the ministry of the church
> may God give you pardon and peace,
> and I absolve you from your sins
> in the name of the Father, and of the Son, +
> and of the Holy Spirit.

> Penitent: Amen.

8. *Proclaiming God's Praise.* After the absolution, the priest continues:

> Give thanks to the Lord, for he is good.
> Penitent: His mercy endures for ever.

9. *Dismissal:* The priest concludes the rite by dismissing the sinner with words like these:

> The Lord has freed you from your sins. Go in peace.

CONFESSIONS

Here is a *sample confession* of a 16-year-old adolescent. Discuss whether you think it is a good confession. Assume that the young man has true sorrow and has examined his conscience.

> Forgive me, Father. I'm a high school student and it has been six weeks since my last confession. What I really notice about myself, Father, is that I can't seem to stand on my own two feet. When the guys go out on weekends, I always seem to drink with them. Sometimes it has gotten out of hand and I know I have said things and done things I wouldn't normally do. I get terribly nasty and later lie to my parents when they ask where I've been and what I've done.

Discuss: 1. Is this a good confession? Does it need improvement? If you said "yes" to the last question, what suggestions would you make?

2. If you were the priest, what would you say to the young man? What penance would you suggest?

In light of the examination of conscience given in the last exercise, write a sample confession for

- a fifth-grade girl (age 10)
- a senior in high school (age 17)
- a married man (age 45)

Discuss the *quality* of the "confessions" in class. Invite a priest to take part in the discussion.

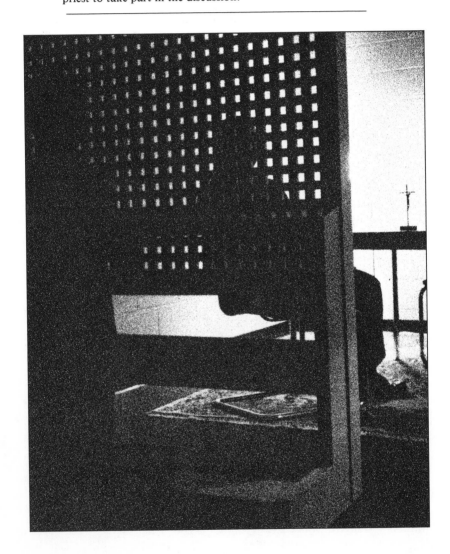

SHOULD YOU USE THIS SACRAMENT?

Should I go to confession? If pollsters are correct, lots of people in recent years are saying no to this question. What a shame, though. The sacrament of reconciliation is the official expression of the church's forgiveness in Christ's name—it is the best way to meet Jesus the Healer who wants to touch us and forgive us so that we can be even closer to him. It can work miracles in our lives if we give it the chance.

What kind of miracles? Well, the miracle of love—a sense that God cares for us because he forgives us and welcomes us back. A sense that God is concerned that we grow, that we get out of our spiritual ruts. But we do need the right attitude. We can't be fearful. Sure, we are all afraid from time to time to admit our failings. It helps to select a confessor who is easy to talk to and to return to him for spiritual guidance. Our attitude should not be one of considering confession just one more thing to do; rather, it should be one of joyous expectation.

Joyous expectation? Yes, we should expect that marvelous things will happen to us in this sacrament. We should expect that the Lord will touch those areas of our lives that keep us shallow, that keep us from growing closer to God and to others. We should expect our Lord to cure us of those failings that we so easily fall into. We should expect our Lord to give us the conviction of heart to begin to uproot our embedded attitudes of selfishness and pride and envy and sloth. We should expect real growth and, because of this expectation, approach the sacrament joyfully.

Catholics—each of us—have a tremendous opportunity to hear our Lord's forgiving voice through his priestly minister. It is up to us to use this great sign of God's love for us. The question remains: "Will we make the effort to grow?"

FORGIVENESS

Reconciliation through this sacrament is the normal way for Catholics to obtain forgiveness. It is the required way for forgiveness of mortal sin. But individuals may receive God's forgiveness for lesser sins through the following means. Check those which you have used in the past.

____ praying directly to God in your own words for forgiveness

____ praying the Our Father

____ donating some money to a less well-off person out of the motivation of love

____ suffering quietly and patiently the joyless tasks of the day and offering it up

____ making a nightly examination of conscience and a promise to do better (firm purpose of amendment)

____ admitting guilt directly to someone we have offended

____ discussing our spiritual progress, including the opening of our conscience, to a prudent and mature lay person for the sake of improvement

____ receiving the Eucharist and trying to live it in our daily life

SUMMARY

1. A healthy acceptance of the reality of sin demonstrates that we need Jesus and his reconciling love.

2. Biblical images of sin include "missing the mark" and "hardheartedness," that is, a failure to love. Sin can be an attitude, an action, a failure to act or a pervasive power that seems beyond individual control.

3. All sin has social consequences and alienates us from God, others and self. Mortal sin kills our relationship with God and others; venial sin is a failure to grow; serious sin rocks the relationship to its foundation.

4. The good news is that Jesus loves sinners.

5. The sacrament of reconciliation has developed through the ages. In the early days public penance received once in a lifetime was the norm. In the Middle Ages private confession as we know it today became the custom. Today the emphasis is on making the sacrament a true sign of healing and bringing out our need to reconcile with the community and God.

6. The sacrament of reconciliation entails contrition, confession of sin, penance and absolution.

EVALUATION

Two of your friends haven't gone to confession in years. It has been so long that they are a bit afraid and don't know what to expect. Based on what you learned in this chapter and your own reflection, prepare a five-minute talk that would ease their fears. Include the following:

1. Why they should go.

2. What is going to take place.

3. Your own attitude to the sacrament.

CLASS PENANCE SERVICE

An excellent way to complete your study of this sacrament would be to plan and participate in this celebration.

1. *Opening Song:* Choose a song like "Day by Day" from *Godspell* or recite a Psalm together, for example, Psalm 100.

2. *Greeting and Mutual Blessing:*

Priest: Peace and grace from God, our Father, and from our Lord Jesus Christ, be with you all!

People: And also with you.

3. *Opening Prayer:* The priest prays for conversion and the grace to repent.

4. *Word of God Proclaimed:*

Reading 1: Dt 6:4-7

Response: Psalm 23

Reading 2: 2 Cor 5:14-21

Alleluia.

R. *Alleluia.*
I am the light of the world. The man who follows me will have the light of life.

R. *Alleluia*

Reading 3: Act out the skit you prepared in number two of the exercise on p. 169. After the play, read Lk 15:11-32.

5. *Homily*

6. *Examination of Conscience:* Use the one on p. 178 or as a class write up your own or meditate and reflect on the Ten Commandments, Dt 5:6-21 and the Beatitudes, Mt 5:3-10.

7. *Rite of Reconciliation:*

    a.   Recite together the Confiteor from Mass.

    b.   Song of peace, for example, St. Francis' "Prayer for Peace"

    c.   Recite together the Our Father

8. *Individual Confession of Sin:*

Choose suitable background music while confessions are taking place.

    a. _____   c. _____

    b. _____   d. _____

9. *Proclaiming God's Mercy:* Magnificat of Mary, Lk 1:46-55 or Psalm 135

10. *Blessing and Dismissal:* Share a symbol of peace and forgiveness with your fellow Christians.

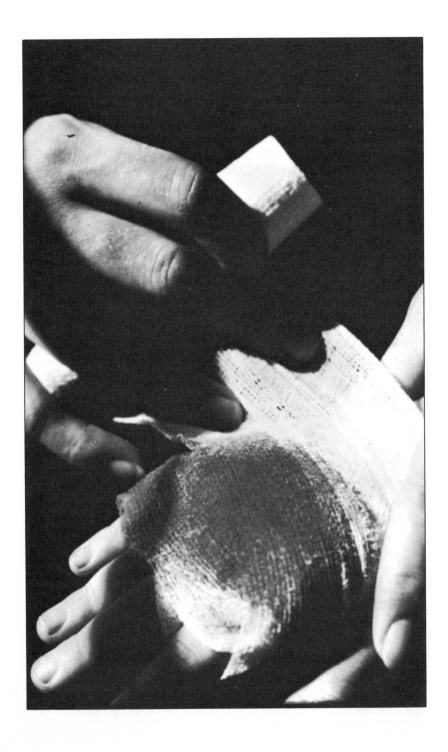

7

Anointing of the Sick—
Our Lord's Healing Touch

If any one of you is in trouble, he should pray; if anyone is feeling happy, he should sing a psalm. If one of you is ill, he should send for the elders of the church, and they must anoint him with oil in the name of the Lord and pray over him. The prayer of faith will save the sick man and the Lord will raise him up again; and if he has committed any sins, he will be forgiven.

—Jas 5:13-15

Do you remember scraping a knee as a child? What did you do? Most of us cried a lot, but we also ran home for mom's comforting touch. There's something revealing here: When we hurt, we need the loving touch of someone to help us cope with the pain. We also need hope. In the novel, *Winning,* the hero of the story is paralyzed from the waist down due to a tragic spinal injury suffered in a football game. His first inclination was to despair, to give up all hope. What pulled him through, though, was the love, encouragement and solidarity of his family, a certain teacher and two friends. He "won" his battle to live a new kind of life because of the support given him.

The sacrament of the sick—anointing—is a sign of comfort, peace, hope and solidarity with others. It also provides a "winning" attitude—the heart and victory of Jesus Christ—in the most painful of human situations: serious illness and near-death. In this chapter we'll study anointing of the sick by discussing suffering, sickness and death and Jesus' help in all of these; by briefly looking at the history, meaning and the ritual of the sacrament; and by

189

discussing how we might live the sacrament in our own lives. Let's begin by examining our own attitudes to suffering and sickness.

ATTITUDE SURVEY

1. Which sickness do you most fear?
   ____ a. terminal bone cancer
   ____ b. congestive heart disease
   ____ c. debilitating, fatal emphysema

2. Which handicap could you most cope with?
   ____ a. inability to talk
   ____ b. total deafness
   ____ c. blindness

3. For whom do you feel the most sorrow?
   ____ a. a retarded child
   ____ b. a totally paralyzed young adult, the victim of a car accident
   ____ c. a senile grandparent, age 70

4. Which statements best describe you? (check two)

   ____ I would never want to suffer terrible pain.

   ____ I can take sickness.

   ____ Physical sickness I could handle; emotional sickness I could not handle.

   ____ I could stand an emotional illness; I could not stand physical sickness.

   ____ I would rather suffer than see a parent suffer.

   ____ I would rather suffer than see a child suffer.

5. Complete these sentences:

   a. What bothers me about human suffering is _____

   _____

   b. If I found out I had cancer, I would _____

   _____

6. *Comment:* "Religion is a source of strength for the sick, suffering and dying."

Share your answers with your classmates.

SICKNESS, SUFFERING AND JESUS

Have you ever been really sick? What did you feel? Miserable, really hurting, very alone? These are some of the things people feel when they come down with a serious or debilitating illness. At times you might even feel that God has abandoned you, that he doesn't love you and that forgiveness isn't yours after all.

These kinds of negative feelings are understandable. Many people cannot understand why our God of love would allow sickness and suffering in his universe, especially when it leads to the suffering of innocent persons. These negative feelings can lead people not to believe in any God at all, certainly not in a loving or personal one.

It was a commonly held belief in our Lord's day that we get sick and suffer because of our sins. This was also an Old Testament belief; for example, Job's friends told him that he suffered his many afflictions because God was punishing him. It is true that *sometimes* we suffer because of our sins. For example, if I drink to great excess (the sin of intemperance), I may end up with a terrible hangover and almost wish that I were dead. Or if I am sexually promiscuous (the sin of fornication), I may end up with a destructive venereal disease. But Jesus taught that suffering and illness cannot simplistically be attributed to sin (see Jn 9:1-3). Good people can suffer, even as Jesus himself suffered when he was unjustly persecuted.

The Jesuit theologian Fr. Karl Rahner has pointed out that the time of grave illness or harsh suffering is a time of an important test. This test places us in the critical situation of making a final decision for God—for his goodness, for his love. But at the same time we are tempted to reject God because we are weak, failing, foolish, worn out, tired and empty. Satan tends to turn us away from God precisely when we are weak and defenseless.

These observations should lead us to two conclusions. First, we should avoid illness as best we can. Because a sickness is a time of temptation, it is basically bad and to be avoided. True, illness and suffering can be an occasion of great spiritual growth, an occasion to grow more deeply loving. But we should never willingly risk turning from God by foolishly subjecting ourselves to grave illness or suffering. Jesus himself did everything he could to cure the sick. For example, he cured the deaf-mute (Mk 7:31-37) and the man born with dropsy (Lk 14:1-6). He gave the power to cure to his apostles (Lk 9:1-2) who performed their healing ministry by laying-on hands and by anointing sick persons with oil (Mk 6:13). These two actions, incidentally, provide the biblical basis for the actions performed in the anointing of the sick.

Our second conclusion should be this: In times of great illness, suffering and even near-death, we need the help of the Lord and other Christians to get us through the illness. We need the strength, support, fellowship and peace of others to help us endure the suffering. We need their encouragement to "offer up" our illness by joining it to Jesus' own sacrifice on the cross so that the powers of evil and sickness (and Satan) can be overcome. The sacrament of the anointing of the sick fills this need.

EXERCISES

1. *Bible Search.* The New Testament provides many examples of Jesus demonstrating his power over sickness. Look up the following passages which exemplify Jesus' healing power. Briefly summarize them and then comment on the meaning of the passage.

Passage	Short Summary	Meaning
Jn 4:46-54	_____	_____
	_____	_____
Mk 1:29-31	_____	_____
	_____	_____
Jn 5:1-15	_____	_____
	_____	_____
Lk 7:1-10	_____	_____
	_____	_____

Mt 9:18-26 _____   _____

_____   _____

Lk 17:11-19 _____   _____

_____   _____

2. *Needing Help.* If you were seriously ill with leukemia and were confined to bed at home, what sorts of problems—emotional, physical, spiritual, mental—do you think you might experience in your last few weeks of life? List four or five of these problems. Then list a specific person who could help you cope with each problem. Discuss briefly how that person could help you.

Problem	*Helper*	*Kind of Help*
a. _____	_____	_____
	_____	_____
b. _____	_____	_____
	_____	_____
c. _____	_____	_____
	_____	_____
d. _____	_____	_____
	_____	_____
e. _____	_____	_____
	_____	_____

3. *Discuss:* "A person should not have to suffer and die alone."

SHORT HISTORY OF THE SACRAMENT

Our short discussion of this sacrament will highlight the New Testament period and the development of the sacrament through the ages.

A. New Testament Times.

1. *Jesus.* People came from all over to be cured by Jesus and Jesus responded to the many requests for healing (Mk 6:56). We

have already seen examples of Jesus' healing ministry in the previous section. We also saw that Jesus gave his power of healing to the disciples who exercised this power even while Jesus was with them (Mk 6:13).

2. *Early Church.* This chapter began with an important quote from the Epistle of James. Reread that quote now. In it, we find ample evidence that the early Christian community had a ceremony very similar to our current rite of the anointing of the sick. We should note two other significant things. First, this action of anointing the sick was performed by the official church through the presbyters (another term for priests). Therefore, these anointings may very well be considered sacraments.

Second, the anointing of the sick was connected to forgiveness of sin. In a sense this sacrament completes the sacrament of reconciliation. In a time of crisis, the person can rely on the church to offer prayer, love and the forgiveness of Christ. As a person prepares for possible death, a time of great loneliness, he or she can experience oneness with the Christian community as it offers strength and reconciliation.

B. Through the Ages.

First to fifth centuries. There is not much evidence discussing this sacrament in the early years. However, this much can be said:

- There was no formal rite.

- The oil was blessed by the official church and was used to anoint the sick. The theme of physical as well as spiritual healing was stressed.

Sixth to eighth centuries.

- Although the oil was blessed by bishops or priests (soon only by the bishop), laymen and laywomen sometimes took the oil home to use when they were sick and administered the sacrament themselves.

- The oil was generously applied to the ailing or injured part of the body. If the sick person had a more general illness, the head, breast or shoulders were anointed. If the theme of sin and forgiveness were to be stressed, the organs of the senses were anointed because these were considered the "gates of sin."

3. *Middle Ages.*

- The anointing became much more ritualized. Only priests were supposed to administer the anointings. This also meant that they had to be much more available to minister to the sick.

- The sacrament was associated more and more with those who were in extreme danger of death. As such, the sacrament was frequently called "extreme unction" (the last anointing) or by the term "sacrament of the departing." This association minimized the use of the sacrament for the sick as it was more and more reserved just for the dying.

4. *Council of Trent to 20th century.* The theology of this important council set the basic tone for the church's practice until recent times. This theology is summarized here:

- Although the sacrament is discussed by Trent in the context of a dying Christian, the administration of the sacrament is *not* limited to those who are at the point of death.

- The sacrament has these purposes and effects:

   —Strengthens and comforts the sick person during the trials of illness.

   —Brings both spiritual and physical healing.

   —Wipes away sin.

- Finally, Trent teaches firmly that this anointing of the sick is truly a sacrament (against the Reformers who denied that it was) and that it is to be administered *only* by a priest.

SERVICE TO THE SICK

One of the corporal works of mercy is "visit the sick." The work flows from Jesus' command to love "the least important of these" (Mt 25:40). Based on this work of mercy, do the following project as a class. First, identify at least three people who are ill—either at home or in the hospital. What are some things these people need? Commit your class to helping these people. Use the space below to jot some notes.

Name of the sick person	Needs	What our class will do to help
1. _____	_____	_____
	_____	_____
2. _____	_____	_____
	_____	_____
3. _____	_____	_____
	_____	_____

Alternative project. Do the same kind of thing for one of the other corporal works of mercy. Again, note the procedure: First, identify a person who needs help; second, find out what the person needs; third, commit yourself to a program of help.

The corporal works of mercy are:

- Feed the hungry.
- Give drink to the thirsty.
- Clothe the naked.
- Visit the imprisoned.
- Shelter the homeless.
- Visit the sick.
- Bury the dead.

INSIGHTS INTO THE SACRAMENT

Our Lord is present in all the sacraments; he comes to us through his special symbols at different times of our lives, especially during those key moments that mean so much. The sacrament of anointing the sick is a wonderful encounter with Jesus. In this sacrament he comes to us as healer, forgiving friend and welcome companion.

Jesus' Healing. Catholics believe that the sacrament of anointing of the sick has some dramatic effects. For one, we believe that our Lord's power may physically heal the person if it is for his or her ultimate good. Most often, though, the sacrament of anointing of the sick gives spiritual strength. What is most needed by the seriously ill, the old and those near death is the strength to hope, to not falter in their love of God. Through the sacrament the church prays that the ill brother or sister may return in health to the rest of the Christian community. But if this is not possible, we pray that our brother or sister may die in the company of the Lord.

The oil used in this sacrament is a most appropriate symbol for healing. Just as we put an ointment on our wounds and burns to heal them, so in this sacrament the blessed oils are administered so that physical and spiritual healing may result. This sacrament is primarily for the sick, a rite of healing. As a result, we should never wait until we are near death to receive it. Anointing does give special strength to the dying, but it is meant to be used by the sick so that they may benefit from the healing power of our Lord.

Forgiveness. Besides healing, the sacrament of the anointing of the sick forgives sins. One of the beautiful effects of the sacrament is the reconciliation of the sick or dying person to God and the Christian community. If possible, the sick person should confess his or her sins. If this is not possible, our Lord's loving forgiveness is still extended to the person. The prayer recited during the rite points to both the theme of healing and the theme of forgiveness:

Through this holy anointing and his great love and
  kindness,
may the Lord fill you with the power of his Holy
  Spirit
In his goodness may he ease your suffering
and extend his saving grace to you,
freed from all the power of sin.

Welcome companion. Our Lord is present to the sick person
through the presence and caring of the Christian community.
What the sick and dying people need very much are friends who
care, who pray for them, who give them the encouragement to join
with Jesus' own suffering and death. The sacrament is a sign of the
Christian community's union with the sick person, especially in
time of miserable pain and even in time of fear of death. The community stands by the side of the sick and dying to reassure them
that God is love, that good can come from suffering, that eternal
life comes after death. Because of the communal support needed
by the sick and dying, the new Rite of Anointing of the Sick (1974)

highly recommends that parishes periodically celebrate communal rites of anointing of the sick. This recommendation is becoming accepted practice in many parishes today.

The Last Rites. You may have seen the term "Viaticum." Holy Viaticum is the reception of Holy Communion by a person who is in serious danger of death. It is a special sign of sharing in the mystery of Jesus' own death and his passage to the Father. Before receiving Viaticum, the dying person confesses (if able to do so) and receives the anointing of the sick. This sacrament is administered within or outside of Mass, and Communion can be received under the species of wine if the person cannot receive the consecrated bread.

EXERCISES

1. In the space below, write a short prayer for a sick or dying person whom you personally know.

2. Explain the different uses of oil in the sacraments of baptism, confirmation and anointing of the sick. Are there similarities? differences?

3. List several reasons why the presence of the Christian community to the sick person is important in this sacrament.

   a. _____   b. _____

   c. _____

4. *Action project.* Find out what is being done in your parish for the sick, the dying, the elderly. Make a report to class. Then, find out from your parish council how you can help in this important ministry. Volunteer your services for a certain period of time.

5. *Liturgical project:* Form a small group and offer to help the parish liturgy team plan a communal celebration of the anointing of the sick.

THE RITE OF ANOINTING OF THE SICK

The following is a very brief summary of the rite for anointing a sick person at the beginning of the danger of death:

1. **Greeting.** The priest greets the sick person and offers God's peace. He may sprinkle the room with holy water. He then reminds those present of the words of the apostle James concerning prayer for the sick, faith, healing and forgiveness (Jas 5:13-16). The sick person is entrusted to the Lord.

2. **Penitential rite.** The priest conducts a penitential rite similar to the one used at Mass. He then reads a brief scripture passage and may or may not give an explanation of its meaning. This is followed by a number of petitions for the sick.

3. **Laying-on of hands.** The laying-on of hands is done in silence.

4. **Anointing of the sick person.** Today the anointing is on the forehead and the hands. The priest says:

> Through this holy anointing
> may the Lord in his love and mercy help you
> with the grace of the Holy Spirit. Amen.
>
> May the Lord who frees you from sin
> save you and raise you up. Amen.

Conclusion. The priest offers a special prayer appropriate to the sick person's condition. All present recite the Our Father and, if the sick person is able to do so, he or she receives Holy Communion. The rite concludes with a special blessing for health, strength, and endurance.

LIVING THE SPIRIT OF THE SACRAMENT

Two modern-day women live the spirit of the sacrament of anointing of the sick. Mother Teresa has spent a lifetime ministering to sick and dying people in the slums of Calcutta, India. She has provided such an example of peace and love that she was awarded the distinguished Nobel Peace Prize. In character, Mother Teresa took the money from the prize and donated it to her mission of mercy. The heroic Dorothy Day also spent her life feeding the sick and poor in the slums of New York.

We too can live the spirit of the sacrament. We can, for example, go out of our way to visit the sick and dying. Do we visit our sick grandparents or other relatives, our lonely neighbors, old folks in nursing homes? By responding to these people we are responding to the Lord. Also, when we go out of our way to help a handicapped person, a retarded adult or child, we are supporting them with the love of Jesus. A final way we show our love is when we respect the basic dignity of a mentally ill person.

When we ourselves are ill, we should look on it as a way for our Lord to take over our lives. We ought to avoid illness whenever possible; but if it should come, we can accept it as an opportunity to overcome selfishness and become more aware of our need for God's help. When we are sick, we can also better understand other people's weaknesses. When we are feeling miserable, we can offer up our feelings to our Lord who suffered for us. Our suffering, when joined with his, can be a power to help bring the love of God into the world.

Discuss: 1. Have you ever grown as a person because of an illness? If yes, why? If not, why not?

2. What do you think when someone makes fun of a handicapped or retarded person?

SUMMARY

1. The sacrament of the anointing of the sick is a powerful meeting of God's love at a difficult time or times in our life.

2. Jesus' ministry extended to the sick; he gave the power of healing to his disciples. The early church followed his example, as testified in the Epistle of James, by anointing the sick, praying for them and forgiving their sins.

3. The sacrament of the anointing of the sick used to be administered by lay persons, but it gradually became the task of the priest. It also became associated only with the dying, though today the original practice has been restored.

4. The sacrament of the anointing of the sick can bring physical healing. It also provides spiritual strength to resist the temptations that come to the sick and dying. Finally, this sacrament forgives sin and provides the strength and encouragement of the Christian community. Hence, it is a powerful symbol of Christ's love.

5. *Viaticum* is the Eucharist given to a dying person. It is administered with confession (if possible) and with the sacrament of the anointing of the sick. Together, these form the "last rites" of the church.

EVALUATION

Suppose you were invited to give a short talk to a group of nurses who work in a hospital. The theme of your talk is the Catholic sacrament of the anointing of the sick. What would you say to them? Write a 300-word essay in response to this question.

OTHER PROJECTS

A. Healing Seminar. Much is written today about physical and spiritual healing. Invite several guests to discuss the meaning of healing. Here are some suggestions:

- a doctor to talk on physical healing
- a psychologist to speak on mental health
- a priest to reflect on spiritual healing

Here are some ideas for further research:

1. Report on what Christian Scientists believe about healing.

2. Show and discuss as a class the movie *The Healing Ministry of the Church* (Pyramid Films).

3. Read and make a report on one of the charismatic books on healing. Here are two famous ones: Francis MacNutt, *Healing* (Notre Dame, Indiana: Ave Maria Press, 1974) and Michael Scanlan, *Inner Healing* (New York: Paulist Press, 1967).

B. Death and Dying: A favorite topic in many high school and college courses in recent years has been the theme of death and dying. One of the functions of the sacrament of anointing of the sick is to ready a person for the passage from this world to the next. You might be interested in doing more research on this topic. Here are some ideas:

1. Write a report on one of these:

   a. What does the bible say about death and the afterlife?

   b. What is the Christian concept of heaven, hell or purgatory?

   c. How does a non-Christian religion view the afterlife?

   d. Pick another Christian religion and describe its "last rites" and their meaning.

2. Describe American funeral practices. Criticize them from a Christian point of view. Interview a funeral director and perhaps a priest.

Alternative: Describe the funeral practices employed in either a very poor country or in a non-Christian culture.

3. Read and report on one of the following books:

Craven, Margaret, *I Heard the Owl Call My Name* (New York: Dell Publishing Co., 1974). A powerful novel about a dying priest. An excellent movie was based on this book.

Kollar, Nathan, *Death and Other Living Things* (Fairfield, N.J.: Cebco Pflaum, 1973). A discussion-type book on the meaning of death from a Catholic perspective.

Kubler-Ross, Elisabeth, ed., *Death: The Final Stage of Growth* (Englewood Cliffs, N.J.: Prentice-Hall, 1975). A series of very good essays on the topic of death.

Kubler-Ross, Elisabeth, *On Death and Dying* (New York: Macmillan, 1972). This is the classic book on the topic. In it, Dr. Kubler-Ross examines the famous five stages of dying.

Moody, Raymond, *Life after Life* (New York: Bantam Books, 1976). A fascinating book which tries to give scientific evidence for life after death.

Morris, Jeannie, *Brian Piccolo: A Short Season* (New York: Dell Publishing Co., 1972). The story of the friendship between the dying Brian and his football buddy Gayle Sayers.

8

Holy Orders—
Call to Service

About this time, when the number of disciples was increasing, the Hellenists made a complaint against the Hebrews: in the daily distribution their own widows were being overlooked. So the Twelve called a full meeting of the disciples and addressed them, "It would not be right for us to neglect the word of God so as to give out food; you, brothers, must select from among yourselves seven men of good reputation, filled with the Spirit and with wisdom; we will hand over this duty to them, and continue to devote ourselves to prayer and to the service of the word." The whole assembly approved of this proposal and elected Stephen, a man full of faith and of the Holy Spirit, together with Philip, Prochorus, Nicanor, Timon, Parmenas, and Nicolaus of Antioch, a convert to Judaism. They presented these to the apostles, who prayed and laid their hands on them.

—Acts 6:1-6

INTRODUCTION

Catholics today are noticing more and more the use of the words *minister* and *ministry* to describe both who they are and what they do. You may have heard expressions like "youth ministry," "eucharistic ministers," "ministry to the aged," "ministers to the separated and divorced," "lay ministry," "priestly ministry," etc. This word *ministry* suggests a very valuable insight which is being emphasized today, namely, that all Christians are special people with a special vocation.

St. Peter writes of our specialness when he says:

> But you are a chosen race, a royal priesthood,
> a consecrated nation, a people set apart to sing the
> praises of God who called you out of darkness into
> his wonderful light (1 Pt 2:9).

By virtue of baptism, all Christians share in the Lord's priesthood. We all share one faith and one mission—to spread the good news of Jesus, to live a life of love, to lead other people to God through prayer, teaching, good example and the like.

The special vocation that goes with our special identity is service. *Minister* means "one who serves." All Christians are called to serve others; all of us are ministers who share in the priesthood of Christ. But different people serve in different ways. Some are called to teach, others to work with the sick. Some are called to witness to their faith in the area of politics, some to bring the witness of love to the business world. Others are called to raise families to walk in the footsteps of Jesus.

Each of us, then, is called to minister. We do it in our own special way, according to our gifts and talents (see St. Paul's words in 1 Cor 12:1-11). All of us are called to holiness because in the church we are one and equal in the Lord, each with a special dignity and each with a special vocation (Eph 4:4-6). We live our lives as married people or single people, as brothers or sisters in religious orders or as priests, with one purpose in mind. How best can we serve God with the gifts, talents and particular call he has given us?

Because this book is on the sacraments, our discussion in this chapter will focus on a special ministry, the sacrament of holy orders. To really appreciate the meaning of this sacrament, though, it was necessary first to talk about ministry. The "ministerial priesthood" is a very special kind of ministry, a special kind of call that has unique meaning for Christians. There is a *sacramental* uniqueness about this particular ministry. Those ordained ministers who are priests respond to God's call to serve in a special way God's people, his ministers. Ministerial priesthood is a sacrament which singles out, anoints, appoints and ordains the "servers of the servers."

The chapter will consider the following themes: (1) the meaning and role of "holy orders"; (2) a short history of this sacrament; (3) some comments on the priestly calling; (4) the rite of ordination for a priest; and (5) some concluding remarks.

EXERCISES

A. *Reflection*

    1. Briefly summarize the key idea behind each of these important Bible passages.

        1 Cor 12:4-11 _____

        _____

        _____

        Mt 28:16-20 _____

        _____

        _____

        1 Cor 3:5-15 _____

        _____

        _____

        Mt 25:31-40 _____

        _____

    2. In light of these New Testament passages, give your own definition of ministry.

        Ministry is: _____

        _____

        _____

    3. Finally, complete this sentence by writing a short essay.

"Given my talents and gifts, I could minister to the Christian community by

_____

_____

_____

_____

B. *Ministry and ministerial priesthood*

Here are some actions—"ministries"—that Christian ministers do. Check (✓) those which you feel a "gifted" Christian can do; put an (X) next to those which are tasks of the "ministerial priesthood," that is, functions of those ordained "to serve the servers."

_____ 1. leading the eucharistic celebrations

_____ 2. taking Communion to the sick

_____ 3. marriage counseling

_____ 4. talking to troubled teens

_____ 5. hearing confessions

_____ 6. teaching religion class

_____ 7. leading people in prayer

_____ 8. anointing the sick

_____ 9. praying over the dead

_____ 10. raising money for the poor

_____ 11. leading a wedding ceremony

_____ 12. keeping parish finances in order

_____ 13. organizing oppressed workers

_____ 14. always being available to talk

_____ 15. participating in Bible study groups

Discussion: Take a look at your list again. In light of your choices, what would you say is the essential "ministry" of the ordained priest?

MEANING OF HOLY ORDERS

People have always needed "mediators" between God and themselves. There has always been a need for men with a special calling to assure us that there is a God who loves us. These mediators with a special calling are called priests.

Every religion has priests or men who serve like priests with special tasks or ministries. In ancient Israel, for example, certain men were called for special tasks. For example, God called Isaiah to preach repentance (Is 6). The shy and reluctant Jeremiah was promised God's own help if he would speak God's message. God asked Hosea to give an example of faithful love through his marriage to Gomer. Amos was called to be *the* prophet of divine justice. Moses was asked to lead Israel out of the land of Egypt, while his brother Aaron was chosen for a different job: to be the priest for Israel. Each of these men was asked to perform a certain task and each had a choice to respond freely to the invitation.

Jesus also made a special call to 12 men from among the many who were his disciples. While others served the Lord in different ways, the special ministry of the twelve was twofold: (1) to make Jesus present in the eucharistic bread and wine of the Last Supper, and (2) to go out into the world with Jesus' own authority to forgive sin and preach his word. Priests today keep this double mission alive by acting as community builders, serving as leaven in the local community to make the word of God live. By the way they live and celebrate the Eucharist, they serve as "light of the world," attracting people to the source of their life—Jesus Christ.

In the early church, men like Peter and Paul recognized that God's plan in Old Testament times and in the time of Jesus' earthly ministry was to call certain men for certain tasks. A replacement for Judas was found. Helpers were chosen to help preach the word. Successors to the apostles had to be appointed. As a result, the early church leaders began to organize the church in the form of a *hierarchy*. A "hierarchical" church suggests that the church is meant to be organized in a certain way, that there are certain ranks and functions in the church which reflect how Jesus wants the members of his body organized. The term "orders" was borrowed from the Roman world and specifically referred to hierarchical organization. When a man receives "holy orders" it means he is consecrated to a certain *position* in a hierarchical church, a position of service and leadership, a position which confers certain responsibilities.

In New Testament times, the authority of handing on the special calling we have been describing was symbolized by the "laying on of hands." There were a number of these special roles in the early church, but the most important ones were those of bishop, priest and deacon. With the laity, bishops, priests and deacons shared in the priesthood of the one and true priest (mediator) between God and us—Jesus Christ. But their participation was in a hierarchical church, a church organized in such a way that certain individuals serve the Lord in special ways for the benefit of the entire community. Through ordination, they receive the special power and authority to minister in the name of Jesus and his church, a ministry that especially includes the following:

- proclaiming the word
- embodying the Gospel in the lives of believers
- leading the community in worship
- healing divisions
- calling people to reconciliation

SOME THOUGHTS ON PRIESTS

Do you agree or disagree with the following statements about the "priestly ministry"? Check (✔) if you agree; mark (0) if you disagree. Share and discuss your responses.

_____ 1. Priests should take an active lead in civil rights movements.

_____ 2. The major role of priests is to show the rest of the people the way to God.

_____ 3. Priests are entitled to receive a "living wage" in line with the people they serve.

_____ 4. The practice of priestly celibacy should be retained.

_____ 5. Priests should be strong leaders.

_____ 6. Priests should stay out of politics.

_____ 7. The major job of a priest is to pray.

THE HIERARCHY TODAY

In the "ministerial priesthood" today, there are different orders or degrees; namely, bishop, priest, deacon. Here is a chart to show how the different functions of the degrees of priesthood compare and contrast. You might read first, though, this important quote from Vatican II's decree on bishops:

Bishops enjoy the fullness of the sacrament of orders, and all priests as well as deacons are dependent on them in the exercise of authority. For the "presbyters" are prudent fellow workers of the episcopal order and are themselves consecrated as true priests of the New Testament, just as deacons are ordained for service and ministry to the people of God in communion with the bishop and his presbytery. Therefore bishops are the principal dispensers of the mysteries of God, just as they are the governers, promoters, and guardians of the entire liturgical life in the church committed to them. (*Decree on the Bishop's Pastoral Office in the Church*, #15).

BISHOP	PRIEST	DEACON
1. Word comes from *episkopoi* which means "overseer"	1. Word comes from *presbyteroi* who were "elders" in the early church and who presided over the Eucharist	1. Word comes from *diakonoi* which means "servers"
2. Successor to the apostles; in union with the pope—the bishop of Rome—and other bishops; is responsible for the welfare of the whole church	2. Helps the bishop; is his extension into the diocese.	2. Today, a "revived" order which can include married and single men of more mature age as well as celibate young men
3. Spiritual "father" of the local church/diocese	3. Presides at Eucharist; leads the people and serves the Lord in re-presenting the sacrifice of the cross	3. Ordained by a bishop; serves him and the people of God by doing the following: • baptizes • anoints the sick • distributes Communion • reads the Bible and teaches • conducts marriages and funerals • administers the "sacramentals" • does many other works of charity • can do church administration work
4. Chief priest and pastor of a diocese	4. Serves the Lord and the community by celebrating the sacraments (except holy orders and usually confirmation)	
5. Symbol of service to the people of God	5. Is symbol by his prayerful witness to the Lord's presence	

6. Minister of all sacraments; the only one who can administer holy orders and is the normal minister of confirmation

6. Preaches and teaches God's word, calling on his blessing for the people

7. Is an active agent for building the Christian community

DISCUSS these questions in small groups. Share your responses later in the larger group.

1. How should you relate to priests today? What do you see as their role?

2. Who is the best priest/bishop/deacon you know? What makes him so good?

3. What do you see as the essential difference between the following:

    • layman
    • priest
    • nun
    • laywoman
    • brother in religious order

4. Should priests (and those in religious life—nuns and brothers and religious order priests) wear distinctive clothing? Why or why not?

SHORT HISTORY OF HOLY ORDERS

In the **early church** there was much variety of ministry. *Overseers* (bishops) were a group of men who led the local church. *Elders* or *presbyters* (priests) helped the apostles, were appointed to help the mission churches (Acts 14:23) and directed local churches in teaching and prayer. They were inducted into office by the laying-on of hands and prayer which invoked the Holy Spirit. *Deacons* served the early Christian communities in many ways, for example, by serving at the Eucharist and preaching God's word. They also were ordained by the laying-on of hands and prayer.

By the **third century** the role of the bishop was firmly established. He had the high priestly service for the flock; he was the symbol of unity. Other priests shared in his priesthood. Clearer lines were drawn between the laity and the clergy, with special emphasis put on the need for priests to live a higher spiritual life and a more perfect moral life. By around the *fifth* century ordination was seen as conveying a special "sacramental character," which meant that once ordained a priest, a man remains a priest forever. Holy orders touches the priest's very being: He is permanently designated by God to be a living sign who points to the Lord and his coming at the end of time.

In the **Middle Ages** the order of diaconate as an active ministry declined. During this period, deacons only assisted at liturgies. Gradually the diaconate was included as only a step on the way to the priesthood. A whole series of "minor orders" was commonly recognized: *porters* (who gathered together the worshipping community), *lectors* (who read God's word), *exorcists* (who assisted the bishop and priests in caring for the catechumens), *acolytes* (who served the deacon and the priest at Mass). In this period, these minor orders—which had their roots in the early church—were widely regarded as merely ceremonial steps to the priesthood. A fifth order, *subdeacon,* was raised to a major order in medieval times because the obligation of celibacy was also required of subdeacons (as it was by now of bishops, priests and deacons). Today, minor orders are called "ministries" and are open to lay people. Only the ministries of lector (reader) and acolyte have been retained. The practice of ordaining subdeacons has been discontinued.

At the **Council of Trent** (16th century) the church fathers reaffirmed that holy orders is a sacrament. Stress was put on the fact that orders conferred on the priestly ministry especially the powers to exercise the ministry of the Eucharist and the forgiveness of sins.

Today, ministerial priesthood is often seen in terms of the images of prophet, priest and king—three roles fulfilled by Jesus the Lord. The prophetic role highlights the word of God through preaching and application to the lives of believers. The priestly role of mediator between God and his people focuses on eucharistic worship. The kingly role is one of a service of leadership in faith, Christian life, prayer and reconciliation. Also, the big theme in the theology of this sacrament today is the fact that *all* the members of God's people share in Christ's priesthood. By living the Eucharist, we bring God to others, especially by extending his love and forgiveness into the world. A priest is a go-between, a mediator between God and people. Baptized Christians share in Jesus' mediation. Ordained priests have the special vocation to serve and build up the *priestly* people. They do so by acting as *leaders* who speak as official representatives of God's word and who lead us in sacramental worship. They direct and assist the building of the community of God's people.

DEACONS

Today the permanent diaconate has been revived and is providing much-needed service to the church and the wider community. Compare the list of what the deacon does in the chart on pages 214-215 with some of the things a deacon did in the early church.

1 Tm 3:8-13 (qualities of a deacon)

Acts 6:1-4

Acts 7 (What did the deacon Stephen do?)

Acts 8:4-13

PRIESTLY CALLING

A vocation. The priesthood is a vocation, just as marriage and the single life are vocations. Vocation means calling, an invitation by the Lord to a special kind of service. Traditionally, young men are said to have the signs of a vocation if they have good health, intellectual ability to do God's work, an upright character to provide good example to God's people and a real desire to serve the Lord and the church through the diaconate or priesthood.

No one, though, has a *right* to ordination. In the last analysis, the church accepts the candidate for this particular service to the church. Ordination does not mean that a given person is "super holy" or that one automatically gets his wishes fulfilled. Ordination means that the church approves of this candidate as one who has received the gift from the Lord to serve his people in the Christian community.

Qualities of the priest. Following are some of the qualities which a good priest has:

a. *He is a man of prayer.* Because he is a leader, his example as a leader in prayer is crucial. Further, he needs the strength of a good prayer life to sustain him in a difficult vocation.

b. *He recognizes that he has come to serve others.* Although a leader in the Christian community, the priest sees his primary contribution as one who serves. He does this by faithfully proclaiming God's message—witnessing to the truth of Jesus' good news. Further, he does it by building community among Christians, celebrating the source of unity in the Eucharist and reconciling people through the sacrament of reconciliation. His service is a sign of our Lord's peace and truth.

c. *He witnesses to God's kingdom.* One of the ways he does this is through the gift of celibacy. Celibacy is the requirement that priests not marry. Stated positively, celibacy is a total commitment of one's life—including one's gift of sexuality—to God and the cause of his kingdom. In the early church, men who were ordained were allowed to marry, but there were always some who did not (see 1 Cor 7:32-35). For around 1,000 years, priests were allowed to take wives and have families. But for the past 10 centuries in the practice of the church, a priest had to take a vow of celibacy. This requirement—a long-standing discipline in the Roman or Latin rite of the Catholic church—has been reaffirmed by Pope John Paul II.

What are the reasons offered for a celibate clergy? St. Paul noted that it helps give a person more freedom to serve Christ. Not having a family to worry about, a priest is both more free to serve others and more able to attach himself wholeheartedly to the Lord. Second, giving up a family is a concrete witness to the sacrifices in the name of the Gospel demanded by Jesus of some of his followers (Mt 19:29-30). Third—and perhaps most important—by living as a loving celibate person, a priest is in reality pointing to eternal life when there will be no marriage. His life is a witness, in the middle of the ordinary affairs and concerns of the world, that we are all destined for union with the Father. Finally, some people point to the witness of Jesus himself who did not marry so that he could be totally involved in doing God's will in serving others.

TO DO

A. *Priesthood and Celibacy*. Is the current church requirement that priests take a vow of celibacy a good discipline? Think this issue out by listing at least four points in favor of a married clergy versus four points in favor of a celibate clergy.

Married clergy   Celibate clergy

1. _____   1. _____

   _____   _____

2. _____   2. _____

   _____   _____

3. _____   3. _____

   _____   _____

4. _____   4. _____

   _____   _____

Discuss: 1. In your judgment, would there be more vocations to the priesthood if there were a married clergy?

2. Interview a parish priest and ask him what he thinks about the role of celibacy in his life.

3. Discuss the meaning of this quote from Matthew's Gospel:

"And everyone who has left houses, brothers, sisters, father, mother, children or land for the sake of my name will be repaid a hundred times over, and also inherit eternal life.

"Many who are first will be last, and the last first" (Mt 19:29-30).

B. *Women and the priesthood.* As you well know, a heated issue both in the church and in society is the proper role of women. This is an important issue, one that demands some study and reflection. Here is a research assignment for you. Do it individually first, then share it with the class. Use the *Catholic Periodical and Literature Index* or a similar research tool to locate at least two articles on the topic of women and the priesthood. At least one article should reflect current church teaching. The other article might well be one which is for the ordination of women. Find the answers to these questions.

1. *References:* (Author, title, magazine/newspaper, date, pages)

    a. _____

    _____

    b. _____

    _____

2. What is the church's official teaching on the issue?

3. What are some arguments for the ordination of women?

4. In light of your reading, where do *you* stand on the issue?

Bonus:

5. Share your research with your mother and ask her opinion on the question.

6. Interview the following for their stand on the issue:

    a. a priest   b. a nun

    c. a grandparent   d. a young woman under 20 years of age

THE RITE OF ORDINATION FOR A PRIEST

1. *INTRODUCTION.* The introductory rites of a typical Mass take place the same as usual up to the homily.

2. *THE CALL TO PRIESTLY MINISTRY.* The deacon of the Mass calls each candidate by name. The response is: "Present." The candidates go before the bishop who receives them after a properly designated priest testifies that they have been trained and are worthy of receiving the sacrament. The bishop then addresses the people and the candidates on the meaning of priesthood.

3. *THE ASSENT TO SERVE.* The bishop now questions the candidates on their willingness to serve.

> Bishop: My sons, before you proceed to the order of the presbyterate, declare before the people your intention to undertake this priestly office.
>
> Are you resolved, with the help of the Holy Spirit, to discharge without fail the office of priesthood in the presbyterial order as conscientious fellow workers with the bishops in caring for the Lord's flock?

Candidates: I am.

> Bishop: Are you resolved to exercise the ministry of the word worthily and wisely, preaching the Gospel and explaining the Catholic faith?

Candidates: I am.

> Bishop: Are you resolved to consecrate your life to God for the salvation of his people, and to unite yourself more closely every day to Christ the High Priest, who offered himself for us to the Father as a perfect sacrifice?

Candidates: I am, with the help of God.

Bishop: Do you promise your Ordinary obedience and respect?

Candidates: I do.

4. *ORDINATION.* When the prayers are concluded, the candidates go and kneel before the bishop who lays hands on them. Then all priests present (wearing stoles) lay their hands on the candidates. The bishop now says the consecratory prayer. Part of the prayer is reproduced here:

Bishop: Come to our help,
    Lord, holy Father, almighty and eternal God;
    you are the source of every honor and dignity,
    of all progress and stability.
    You watch over the growing family of man
    by your gift of wisdom and your pattern of order.
    When you had appointed high priests to rule your
       people,
    you chose other men next to them in rank and
       dignity
    to be with them and to help them in their task;
    and so there grew up
    the ranks of priests and the offices of levites,
    established by sacred rites.

    In the desert
    you extended the spirit of Moses to seventy wise
       men
    who helped him to rule the great company of his
       people.
    You shared among the sons of Aaron
    the fullness of their father's power,
    to provide worthy priests in sufficient number
    for the increasing rites of sacrifice and worship.
    With the same loving care
    you gave companions to your Son's apostles
    to help in teaching the faith:
    they preached the Gospel to the whole world.

    Lord,
    grant also to us such fellow workers,
    for we are weak and our need is greater.

    Almighty Father,
    grant to these servants of yours
    the dignity of the priesthood.
    Renew within them the Spirit of holiness.
    As co-workers with the order of bishops
    may they be faithful to the ministry
    that they receive from you, Lord God,
    and be to others a model of right conduct.

    May they be faithful in working with the order of
       bishops,
    so that the words of the Gospel may reach the ends
       of the earth,

and the family of nations,
made one in Christ,
may become God's one, holy people.

We ask this through our Lord Jesus Christ, your
    Son,
who lives and reigns with you and the Holy Spirit,
one God, for ever and ever.

R. Amen.

The ordination ceremony concludes with the vesting of the new priests with chasubles, anointing of the hands with chrism, the presentation of a chalice filled with water and wine and the exchange of a sign of peace.

5. *LITURGY OF THE EUCHARIST.* The Mass concludes as usual, but celebrated with the bishop, the fraternity of priests present and the newly ordained priests.

EXAMINATION

As a class, prepare a list of the five most important questions you think should be asked of a man before he is ordained. Compose this list from the perspective of a young person who is really concerned about church leadership.

1. _____   4. _____

   _____   _____

2. _____   5. _____

   _____   _____

3. _____

   _____

CONCLUDING REMARKS

As we have seen in this chapter, holy orders is a sacrament administered for the three roles of deacon, priest and bishop. The permanent diaconate especially is a phenomenon of today's church. Many married men are accepting the call to serve the church in an ordained capacity, both as ministers of the word and as living examples of brotherly service.

You are probably aware, too, that there are two general types of priests: diocesan (or secular) and those in religious orders. Diocesan priests usually staff parishes and are directly under the authority of the local bishop. They receive a small salary with which to support themselves. Many diocesan priests do other kinds of work, too, but most of them are in parishes. Priests in religious orders like the Jesuits or Franciscans make vows of poverty, chastity and obedience to their local superiors. Each religious community was founded to do a special kind of work. Members live a communal life—praying, working and recreating together. They try to remain free enough to go wherever the universal church needs them.

Even though they are not ordained, a number of men and women live a life bound to religious orders. Communities of women (sisters, nuns) and communities of men (brothers) also live a common life of prayer and of service to the church. Individuals in these "religious communities" also take the vows of poverty, chastity (celibacy) and obedience. They seek to serve the Lord and the church and to be a sign to the rest of the world that we are all destined for Christ. They, too, have special ministries (for example, education, care of the sick, care of orphans, etc.) and wear distinctive clothes (called "habits") to mark them off as especially committed to God.

Those ordained or in religious life are Christians like all of us. They are not "better" nor do they claim to be better than the laity. As St. Paul said, we are all one in the Lord. Their vocation is to witness in a special, serving way to the good news that is happening in our midst. They remind us by their love and style of life that ours is a God who cares for us and who has great things in store for us.

Perhaps the Lord is calling you to serve him in the priesthood or as a member of a religious order. Now is the time of your life to listen to any promptings you may have. Examine your talents. Ask God what he wants you to do to serve him best. Pay attention to any urgings you might have. Discuss your thoughts (and fears) with an adult you admire and trust, perhaps a priest, brother or sister. They, too, had to make a decision to follow a call. Perhaps their personal story will help you decide what God has in store for you.

RESEARCH

1. Research the history of one religious order. Do this by reading or interviewing a member of the order. Find out the following information:

   a. Who founded the order and when? _____
   _____

   b. Why was the order founded—what work did it originally do? _____
   _____

   c. Which countries has it worked in? _____
   _____

   d. Was the order ever persecuted? _____
   _____

   e. How many members does the order have

      (1) internationally? _____

      (2) in your local community? _____

      f. What work is the order involved in today? ___

      _____

      g. Has the order undergone a "renewal" since Vatican II? If so, what changes were made? ___

      _____

      h. (Optional)—If you interviewed someone for this assignment, ask him or her why he or she joined this order rather than another one.

2. Invite to class several representatives of religious orders (and a representative of the diocesan clergy) and have them report on the special spirituality of their vocation—how they pray, what they see as their main work, what binds them in community, etc.

Some examples

Carmelites	Franciscans
Dominicans	Benedictines
Jesuits	Sacred Hearts

SUMMARY

1. All of us are called to ministry, a life of service to others. Holy orders is a special, sacramental ministry of service to the Christian community.

2. "Holy orders" refers to the consecration of a man to a certain position of service in a hierarchical church.

3. Those who are ordained perform the following tasks: proclaim God's word; plant the Gospel in the lives of believers; lead the community in worship; heal divisions; and call people to reconciliation.

4. The bishop is the symbol of unity in the church; priests and deacons are united to the bishop and extend his ministry to God's people.

5. One way to view the priesthood today is in terms of the kingly role of service to God's people, the prophetic role of

preaching God's word and the priestly role of mediating God's presence, especially in the Eucharist.

EVALUATION

Suppose a Protestant friend of yours engaged you in a discussion of the priesthood. Her belief is that because every Christian is a minister of some kind, there is no need for a special priesthood. In light of what you have read in this chapter, respond to her argument. Write a page or so response to her in your journal.

A COUPLE OF PROJECTS

1. Interview the vocation director of your diocese. Ask him or her what one must do to enter the religious life. Discuss the signs of a vocation. Ask about the type and kind of seminary training in your diocese. As an alternative, interview the local vocation director of one of the religious orders working in your diocese. Ask the same kind of questions and share your findings with your classmates.

2. Research what another Christian body believes about ministry/priesthood. You may wish to interview a minister or lay leader in one of these denominations:

> Baptist
>
> Lutheran
>
> Episcopalian
>
> Presbyterian
>
> Methodist

9

Marriage—
Sacrament of Love and Life

Then Jesus said to them
". . .But from the beginning of creation God made them male
and female. This is why a man must leave father and mother,
and the two become one body. They are no longer two,
therefore, but one body. So then, what God has united, man
must not divide."

—Mk 10: 5-9

INTRODUCTION

You are probably going to get married someday. Most people do. But if you read the newspapers or listen to talk shows you know that marriage is getting a bad press today. For many people marriage is bad news. They feel trapped and ill-prepared. They are unhappy. They break up. In fact, the divorce rate in many parts of the country is close to one out of two marriages. Children who result from these unhappy marriages are themselves often unhappy.

But this chapter is not about the bad news that is going around about marriage today. On the contrary, the Gospel of Jesus tells us that marriage is good news. In fact, marriage is a sacrament. As a sacrament, a sign of God's incredible love for us, marriage is an ongoing sign of Jesus' presence to the husband and wife. It really is fantastic news to know that day in and day out a couple have the love of the Lord to sustain them in sorrow and joy, in bad times as well as in good times. Because marriage is a sacrament of God's grace, it really is great news that the husband

and wife bring Christ and his good news of love, forgiveness and unity to each other.

What is it that makes marriage totally different from any other human relationship? Someone once said that there are two things that distinguish marriage from other relationships. First, marriage is a process whereby *I* becomes *we*. The individuals in the relationship grow together as a couple who also make room for God and children. Beginning as two "ones," they grow together in a community of love. Second, marriage is a lifelong growth from romantic love to committed love. For a successful life of love together, the couple grow from an overpowering romantic fascination with each other to an overwhelming commitment to be faithful and true, to a commitment to share everything about themselves with each other—with no strings attached.

Christian marriage goes by the name of the sacrament of matrimony. We'll take a look at this sacrament by reflecting on what it means for God to bless human marriage. Then, after a short review of the history of the sacrament, we'll reflect a bit on the beautiful theology of matrimony. Finally, there will be a brief look at the rite of the sacrament, followed by some pointers on how you can prepare today for a successful Christian marriage. But let's begin with our usual exercises.

SOME STARTERS

A. *Love and Marriage.* Here are some statements people make about both love and marriage. Rank-order them according to which statement you think is most true (1) to which statement you think is least descriptive of love or marriage (5).

1. Love is primarily

____ a commitment

____ a feeling

____ a sharing

____ instinctual

____ spiritual

2. When I hear the word "love" I think of

____ my parents

____ sex

____ a good friend

____ marriage

____ being accepted

3. Marriage is

_____ give and take (a
50-50 deal)

_____ unrealistic today

_____ only for those
who want kids

_____ a special way to
grow together

_____ a sure way to lose
your freedom

4. Marriage as a sacrament
means that

_____ the partner is the
primary means to
holiness

_____ two become one
in Christ

_____ being blessed with
children is an im-
portant sign of
God's love

_____ God blesses a cou-
ple's sexuality in a
profound way

_____ a couple must re-
main faithful to
each other forever

B. *Successful marriage.* Which of the following do you think
are essential ingredients for a successful marriage? Mark a
check (✔) if you agree with the statement about a particular requirement for a good marriage; mark an (X) if you
don't agree with it as necessary. Leave the space blank if
you don't know.

____ 1. People who marry should have the same general interests: intellectual, recreational and social.

____ 2. Married people should have the same religion.

____ 3. For a successful marriage, couples ought to agree
on money matters.

____ 4. Good relations with in-laws are essential for a happy marriage.

____ 5. People who marry should agree on sex roles and the
number of children *before* they marry.

____ 6. Respect for the other is a key to a good marriage.

____ 7. The age of the couple when they marry is a good
predictor of the success of the marriage.

____ 8. A disagreement before marriage will probably be a
problem after marriage.

____ 9. Children are essential to a happy marriage.

____ 10. A couple who prays together will have a better
chance for a good marriage.

C. *Sharing.* Share your responses with your classmates. Then together complete the following:

Love in marriage is _____

_____

The essential ingredient for a successful marriage is _____

_____
_____

MARRIAGE AS SACRAMENT: SOMETHING SPECIAL AND HOLY

There is nothing as ordinary as love and marriage. People everywhere get married. You can find married people in every nation, from every religious and racial grouping and from diverse social and economic backgrounds. Husbands and wives everywhere experience the same kinds of things: the joys of lovemaking, impatience with each other's faults, the daily "grind" of going to work or taking care of the house, the thrill of a first baby, the sadness of a child who leaves home, growing old together. Marriage, like friendship, is a universal human relationship.

Catholics believe, however, that in the midst of the ordinariness of marriage there is something special and unique about it. They believe that Jesus sanctified marriage and thus made it a sign of God's love for men and women. They believe that marriage is a special, holy sign that brings about the love it symbolizes.

God loves us as we are. By making marriage a sacrament, our Lord is saying something profound. He is saying, in effect, that his Father loves us the way we are, especially in the ordinary and common vocation of marriage. Of course, the Father also said he loved us the way we are as humans by sending his only Son to be our brother. But he says it again and somewhat differently in marriage.

What does marriage-as-sacrament say? Among other things it says this: Sex is holy. Sex is also fun and playful. Sex celebrates our differences while at the same time it brings together man and woman in the most intimate of ways. In addition, sex brings children. But again, sex is holy. What this means is that God delights in the humans he has created, in the fun and playfulness and differences and the children which our sexuality celebrates. Sex is not evil and wicked and dirty, though people do evil and wicked and dirty things with it. Sex is holy. Genesis says it best:

> God created man in the image of himself,
>   in the image of God he created him,
>   male and female he created them.

> God blessed them, saying to them, "Be fruitful, multiply, fill the earth and conquer it. . . ." (Gn 1:27-28).

> God saw all he had made, and indeed it was very good (Gn 1:31).

Thus, when men and women love in marriage they are a real symbol of God's love. If God loves us as we are and has blessed our sexuality, in Christian marriage we have a special sign of God's love. That love rests in the love of the husband for the wife and the wife for the husband. When one partner loves the other, he or she is demonstrating in a real way the love of God. Each partner can become the way to the Father for the other. As St. John wrote, "God is love" (1 Jn 4:8). There is something very important in this insight. The married love of the husband and wife is a *sacrament* of God's love—it makes visible what is invisible, tangible what is intangible. St. Paul saw it this way:

> . . .and follow Christ by loving as he loved you . . . (Eph 5:2).

> Wives should regard their husbands as they regard the Lord. . . (Eph 5:22).

> Husbands should love their wives just as Christ loved the church and sacrificed himself for her (Eph 5:25).

God is present when man and woman love in marriage. When husband and wife give of themselves in sexual love, in the friendship of just "being together," in the forgiveness of daily faults, in doing the extra without asking for a return, God's love is both symbolized and made present. In Christian marriage, wherever love is—whether it be sexual love, friendship love or heroic and committed love—there God is. Thus, in marriage husband and wife are a source of God's grace and love. They give the gift of Jesus' love to each other because in the sacrament of matrimony he has promised to give himself to them every minute of their married life.

A marriage blessed with children is a special sign of God's love. Ideally, a child is the result of a mother and father's love. When a Christian marriage is blessed with children, the mother and father have shared in God's own creative power. They have *procreated,* that is, cooperated with God in bringing forth new life. Most parents will tell you that there is not a greater joy or mystery in life than to participate in God's own creative act of bringing forth new human life. This participation is a special sign—a holy and beautiful sign—of God's love. It is a concrete sign—a new life—of God's love and the love of the parents. Children themselves are a kind of living sacrament because they *point to* the love of God as lived in their parents. At the same time, they *are* the result of God's love as lived through the parents.

In summary, we can surely affirm that the ordinary human relationship of marriage is indeed special and holy. Marriage is holy because our God says sex is holy. Marriage is a sacrament because God's love is made present through husband and wife and their love is sustained because of Jesus' presence. Christian marriage is special because in it a couple shares God's own creative power in bringing forth new life.

THINGS TO DO AND CONSIDER

A. *What Scripture Says About Love and Marriage.* Below are listed the possible readings used in the Rite of Marriage. Divide into several groups. Each group should be responsible for one or two readings from each category by doing the following:

1. Read carefully each of the passages.

2. Briefly summarize the main points.

3. Prepare a five-minute homily based on these particular readings for the rest of the groups. One person will deliver it.

Old Testament Readings

1. Creation of man and woman (Gn 1:26-28, 31a)

2. Creation of woman (Gn 2:18-24)

3. Meeting of Isaac and Rebekah (Gn 24:48-51; 58-67)

4. Marriage of Tobias and Sarah (Tb 7:9c-10, 11c-17)

5. Prayer of new spouses (Tb 8:4-9)

6. Love as strong as death (Song of Songs 2:8-10, 14, 16a; 8:6-7a)

7. A good wife (Sir 26:1-4, 16-21)

8. A new covenant (Jer 31: 31-32a, 33-34a)

New Testament Readings

1. Love of Christ (Rom 8, 31b-35, 37-39)

2. Christian life (Rom 12: 1-2, 9-18)

3. Temples of the Holy Spirit (1 Cor 6:13c-15a, 17-20)

4. Love (1 Cor 12:31-13:8a)

5. Marriage (Eph 5:2a, 21-33)

6. Live in love (Col 3:12-17)

7. Family peace and harmony (1 Pt 3:1-9)

8. Real and active love (1 Jn 3:18-24)

9. God is love (1 Jn 4:7-12)

10. Marriage of the Lamb (Rv 19:1, 5-9a)

Gospel Readings

1. Beatitudes (Mt 5:1-12a)

2. Salt and Light (Mt 5:13-16)

3. House on a rock (Mt 7: 21, 24-29)

4. Man must not divide what God has united (Mt 19:3-6)

5. Love, the great commandment (Mt 22:35-40)

6. Two become one body (Mk 10:6-9)

7. Cana (Jn 2:1-11)

8. Remain in love (Jn 17: 20-26)

9. Love as Jesus loved (Jn 15:12-16)

10. Prayer for unity (Jn 17: 20-26)

B. *Love.* Jesuit Father John Powell, one of today's best Catholic authors, has written a number of beautiful books on love. In one of them entitled *The Secret of Staying in Love,* Father Powell discusses seven theses about true love. Here they are with a very brief explanation of each. Think of a close friend while you read each one and mark on the continuum where you are in your relationship with that person right now. Five means that this thesis perfectly describes your relationship; 1 means that you have a long way to go.

1. *Love is not a feeling.* Feelings change too much for love to be based on them. Feelings might start off a love relationship but they cannot sustain it.

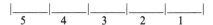

2. *Love is a decision-commitment.* Love involves primarily giving, not receiving. It is a decision to spend time with and follow through on responsibilities made to the loved one. It takes work.

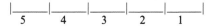

3. *Effective love is unconditional.* True love is love with no strings attached. Unconditional love is caring for a person for the way he or she is, not the way I want him or her to be.

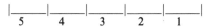

4. *Love is forever.* True love does not waver. No condition of time is put on it.

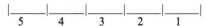

5. *Commitment of love involves decisions.* If I love you, I must feel responsible for your life, growth and the development of all your human powers.

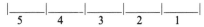

6. *The essential gift of love is a sense of personal warmth.* The great gift of love is that I help you love yourself.

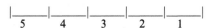

7. *Love means the affirmation, not the possession of the one loved.* True love allows the loved one the freedom to be himself or herself.

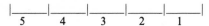

Discuss:

1. Do you think these theses describe marital love, too? Would you want your marriage partner to understand love the same way as Father Powell does? Why or why not?

2. Compare Father Powell's theses with what St. Paul wrote in 1 Cor 12:31-13:8a.

3. You may wish to read and discuss one of Father Powell's books. Here are four excellent ones: *Why Am I Afraid to Love?, Why Am I Afraid to Tell You Who I Am?, The Secret of Staying in Love, Unconditional Love.* You might also enjoy reading his short book, *He Touched Me,* about his relationship with Jesus. All of these are published by Argus Communications.

4. Do the theses above describe Jesus' relationship with you? your relationship with him? Discuss.

SACRAMENT OF MARRIAGE THROUGH THE AGES

New Testament times. Our brief survey of the history of this sacrament must begin with Jesus' attitude toward marriage. For Jesus, marriage was sacred. He restored the ideal of marriage which God intended from the beginning when he said: "So then, what God has united, man must not divide" (Mt 19:6). Marriage between man and wife was to be like God's *covenant of love* for his people: constant, faithful and forever. Furthermore, Jesus greatly supported women in marriages. In the Judaism of his day, a wife had very few rights if her husband was unfaithful to her. But Jesus made women equal to men in marriage when he said: "The man who divorces his wife and marries another woman is guilty of adultery against her" (Mk 10:11).

Though he himself did not marry, Jesus performed his first miracle at a wedding feast. His presence at Cana surely showed that he enjoyed wedding celebrations. His sensitivity to the young couple was one concrete way he blessed marriage.

St. Paul also had a number of things to say about marriage. Among his important teachings were that a husband and wife make a lifelong commitment when they marry (1 Cor 7:10-11) and that they should love each other as Jesus loved us (see Eph 5). If they do so, they are a sacrament, a sign of the loving Savior who died for us.

In the early centuries. In the early centuries, there was no specific liturgy for marriage. Marriage was seen as a civil and family affair with Christian significance. St. Augustine wrote about marriage as a sign, a sacrament of the relationship between Christ and his church. This relationship was marked by undying fidelity. Thus, while the civil law could allow divorce, it was generally held in this period that divorce did not apply to Christians who were called to lifelong faithfulness in marriage.

Also, during this period, church teachers had to defend the right of people to marry. Some heretics taught that anything connected with sex was filthy, dirty and the result of sin and the influence of the devil. Although St. Augustine rightly defended the virtues of marriage, he tended to overemphasize that in marriage only sexual intercourse with the intention of having children was morally justifiable. He thought that original sin had so affected human sexuality that intercourse always carried with it some moral evil.

During the Middle Ages. Theologians of this period echoed Augustine's teaching that marital love should be primarily for procreation. They also saw marriage more in terms of *contract* than covenant as it had been described earlier. Speaking of marriage as contract enabled church people to describe very precisely what was meant by a "valid" marriage and "marital consent," what were the marital duties of each partner, etc. What was lost in this period, however, was the rich notion of marriage as covenant. This period in church history clearly defended marriage as a sacrament that made objectively present in the husband and wife the invisible union of Jesus and his church.

Council of Trent to today. Because most Protestants stressed only baptism and Eucharist as true sacraments, the church had to state firmly that marriage was a sacrament intended by Christ (and as taught in Ephesians). Every marriage between baptized persons is a sacramental marriage which lasts until the death of one of the partners. Divorce was not allowed, although a declaration of nullity was permitted when it was shown that there had been no real Christian marriage from the very beginning (for example, when no true consent was given). Nullity simply means that church courts determined that there was no marriage to begin with.

Today, there are two striking developments in the sacrament. The first is that "procreation of children" is not talked about as the only purpose of marriage. Rather, now the church speaks of two aims that exist together: the sharing of love and affection between husband and wife and the procreation of children. This important distinction makes it clear that the pleasure in sexual

lovemaking is not just something that is tolerated because of the ultimate goal of procreating children. The joy of sexual sharing—which ought to bring a couple even closer together—is one of the purposes of marriage itself. Their union is a sign, a sacrament of Christ's union with his church.

Second, because of psychological insights into the human personality, the church has recognized more and more in some cases that what appeared to be Christian marriage in the beginning simply never was. Hence, many Catholics notice today that there have been more and more annulments of marriages. Annulments are not divorces with remarriage. The church rightly teaches that she cannot dissolve a true Christian marriage and grant a person the right to remarry. Jesus himself forbade divorce and remarriage. But she can declare that what appeared to be a true marriage in Christ never really was because of some impediment or psychological condition of one of the parties.

MARRIAGE LAWS

To test your knowledge of the marriage laws of the church, here are some true and false statements. See how much you know by trying your hand at these. The correct answers will be given on page 247.

_____ 1. A Catholic may not marry a non-Catholic.

_____ 2. A Catholic must marry before a priest and two witnesses.

_____ 3. The church encourages a couple to live together before getting married.

_____ 4. The Catholic church recognizes homosexual marriages.

_____ 5. Catholic church teaching holds that marriage is always permanent.

_____ 6. The church will bless a marriage where the couple has decided beforehand not to have any children.

_____ 7. The church hopes each married couple will have as many children as possible.

_____ 8. A Catholic is obliged to obey church laws on marriage.

_____ 9. There are no restrictions—besides state laws—for two Catholics who wish to marry.

THEOLOGY OF MARRIAGE

In recent years, the theology of marriage has received a lot of attention. Some of the rich insights discussed by theologians about Christian marriage are treated here.

Marriage as sign. As we have seen earlier, Christian marriage is a special kind of sign, a sacrament. In a way, a married couple is a symbol of the church. Christian marriage is, in fact, the church in miniature. As Christ loves his people (the church) totally and unconditionally and the church responds to that love, so the husband and wife love each other. Their love is a sign of God's love for us.

Marriage as covenant. Unconditional love is love with no strings attached. Unconditional love is love that knows no bounds—it lasts forever, is freely given and weathers all kinds of hardships: sickness, poverty, etc. Another term for the unconditional love given in matrimony is covenantal love.

Marriage described as covenant differs from marriage as contract. In a contract, a person gives in order to get. This sometimes is expressed by the cliche that marriage is a 50-50 proposition (see Diagram 1). But this description is weak. Note on what little ground the relationship rests. If one or the other partner does not give 50 percent (the agreed-upon terms of the contract), the relationship rests on weak footings and is more likely to fail.

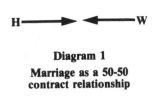

Diagram 1

Marriage as a 50-50 contract relationship

Covenant is a much richer way to describe marriage. It goes back to Old Testament times when God made a covenant with Noah (Gn 9:8-17) to continue life on earth; with Abraham (Gn 15, 17) to bless him with land and a people; with Moses (Ex 6:7) to make Israel a holy nation; with David (2 Sm 7:14) to establish firmly a blood relationship with his people, a relationship written on the heart (Jer 31:33). In the New Testament, Jesus' blood is described as the blood of the new covenant (Mk 14:24). He is the sign of our salvation and the cause of it.

Covenant is an open-ended contract. It demands 100 percent effort by both parties. Just as God was always faithful to his commitment of love even though the Jews often turned away from his love and kindness, so the husband and wife are to be faithful to each other in marriage. Their relationship can be illustrated as follows:

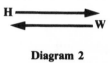

Diagram 2
Marriage as covenant:
100% giving

Note in this relationship that neither party holds back. There is a commitment that, come "hell or high water," both parties will try to give 100 percent. If one party should fail temporarily and give only 60 percent or 40 percent, the relationship still stands on firm ground because the total commitment is there. In a marriage seen as covenant, partners do not nitpick on what was done in the past or who gave what to the relationship. Rather, the concern is on the present and the future: What can I do today to love my spouse as God loves his children?

Some things follow from the insight that marriage is a covenant of love. First, it is *creative*. Marriage is open to the procreation and education of children. This openness helps married and family love to grow and increase.

Second, married love *unites* the couple in an even closer bond of love. When "no strings are attached" to the relationship, the couple can trust each other totally and can give themselves without holding back. This kind of love—which is truly covenantal—reflects the union between Jesus and his people.

Third, the ministers of the sacrament of matrimony are the couple themselves. The sign of the marriage sacrament is not a formula of words with some symbol like water or oil. Rather, it is the mutual promise of the husband and wife to be faithful to each other forever. This sign continues as the couple lives out their promise. This means that each time they love—are tender, considerate, patient, forgiving, etc.—Jesus becomes present in their midst, the Spirit dwells in their hearts. Because this is true, we can see why marriage is truly a sacrament, a sign of and cause of God's grace. Whenever the husband and wife love they are both a source of grace to each other and help reveal God's love to each other and everyone they meet.

Marriage is a beautiful sacrament!

___

GOOD REASONS FOR MARRIAGE

Check any of the following which you think are good reasons for marriage. Discuss with your classmates those which you think help lead to bad marriages.

_____ to escape the hassles of one's parents

_____ to escape boredom

_____ because I love the other for himself or herself

_____ because I'm getting too old and maybe nobody will have me later

_____ because the other will "fulfill" me as a person

_____ because I need someone

_____ so I can enjoy sex without feeling guilty

_____ because of pregnancy

_____ because I want to love my partner wholeheartedly

_____ because he or she is good looking

_____ because my friends are getting married

_____ to have children together

_____ to escape loneliness

_____ because I feel called to serve my friend forever

_____ because it would be difficult to live without the other

Answers to Quiz on Page 243

1. False. Although "mixed marriages" can bring problems to the faith-life of a couple, the local bishop can and does permit Catholics to marry non-Catholics. The couple is counseled on the problems involved in such a marriage.

2. True. This is the "canonical form" of marriage which follows church law. Exceptions can be made by the local bishop.

3. False.

4. False. There really is no such thing because "true" marriage can only be between a man and a woman.

5. True

6. False. A marriage must be open to the procreation and education of children just as it must always be open to mutual love and sharing between the couple.

7. False. Parents must plan families using moral means and taking into consideration many factors including finances, health of the parents, present size of the family, etc.

8. True.

9. False. For a valid Catholic marriage, the couple must be of age, never before validly married, freely intend to live together until death, be capable of sexual intercourse and not closely related by blood or marriage.

RITE OF CHRISTIAN MARRIAGE

I. *INTRODUCTORY RITE AND LITURGY OF THE WORD.* This proceeds as usual with the readings taken from those listed on pages 236-237.

II. *RITE OF MARRIAGE*

A. *Introduction.* The priest addresses the bride and groom:

My dear friends, you have come together in this church so that the Lord may seal and strengthen your love in the presence of the church's minister and this community. Christ abundantly blesses this love. He has already consecrated you in baptism and now he enriches and strengthens you by a special sacrament so that you may assume the duties of marriage in mutual and lasting fidelity. And so, in the presence of the church, I ask you to state your intentions.

B. *Statement of Intentions.* Priest questions the couple:

N. and N., have you come here freely and without reservation to give yourselves to each other in marriage?

Will you love and honor each other as man and wife for the rest of your lives?

Will you accept children lovingly from God, and bring them up according to the law of Christ and his church?

(The couple answer the questions separately.)

C. *Consent.* The priest invites the couple to declare their consent.

Priest: Since it is your intention to enter into marriage, join your right hands, and declare your consent before God and his church.

(They join hands.)

Groom: I, N., take you, N., to be my wife. I promise to be true to you in good times and in bad, in sickness and in health. I will love you and honor you all the days of my life.

Bride: I, N., take you, N., to be my husband. I promise to be true to you in good times and in bad, in sickness and in health. I will love you and honor you all the days of my life.

D. *Reception of Consent.* The priest receives their consent for the whole church:

You have declared your consent before the church. May the Lord in his goodness strengthen your consent and fill you both with his blessings. What God has joined, men must not divide.

People: Amen.

E. *Blessing and Exchange of Rings.* At this point in the ceremony, the rings are blessed and lovingly exchanged by the couple. The ring is a symbol for eternal love.

III. *LITURGY OF THE EUCHARIST.* The marriage Mass continues pretty much as usual with a few minor changes.

A. After the Lord's Prayer, the priest faces the couple and gives a beautiful *nuptial blessing.* He praises God for his divine plan of creation in his image and likeness, for the beauty of marital love and marriage which symbolizes Christ's love for his church. Then he prays specifically for the couple that they might love and cherish each other for life.

B. The rite concludes with the following blessing:

May God, the almighty Father,
give you his joy
and bless you in your children. *Response:* Amen.

May the only Son of God have mercy on you
and help you in good times and in bad. *Response:* Amen.

May the Holy Spirit of God
always fill your hearts with his love. *Response:* Amen.

And may almighty God bless you all,
the Father,
the Son, + and the Holy Spirit. *Response:* Amen.

A WEDDING

If you get the chance, try to attend a wedding of a relative or friend. Make a report to the class treating some of the following points:

1. Brief description of the ceremony.
2. Was it a formal or informal wedding? Did you like it?
3. What was the theme of the readings and homily?
4. Did anything special happen at the wedding not listed in the rite? Did you like it?
5. Any other comments?

PREPARING FOR MARRIAGE

Most of us will get married one day. Is there anything we can do now to prepare for that sacrament? Here are a few suggestions that might help.

Cultivate friendships. The basis of any good marriage is friendship. Sexual love is certainly important in marriage, but for the long run friendship is what counts. Friendship love is characterized by common interests and spending time together. In addition, friendship love does not distort reality like "puppy love" or infatuation can. A friend recognizes the truth about the other person but is willing to accept the other despite his or her flaws. Finally, friends learn to *give* wholeheartedly to the relationship, seeking the other's good over their own. If you want to prepare for a good marriage, make friends now and learn how to keep them.

Learn how to communicate. Friendship and marriage are built on communication—a coming into unity, a oneness. Communication is a two-way process. The first part of the process involves the risk of sharing not only your thoughts but also your deepest feelings. For example, to be able to say "I love you" to a friend and mean it takes courage and trust that the other will accept your offer of love. The second part of the communication process involves really *listening* to the other, listening not only to the words used but to the nonverbal communication as well. A large part of the message a person communicates is conveyed in body language: through gestures, expressions, body posture, eye contact and the like. A sensitive person will learn how to "read" and interpret these kinds of nonverbal cues.

Be forgiving. What cements human relationships together more than any other ingredient is forgiveness. Friends hurt friends; husbands and wives sometimes hurt each other. This happens accidentally and sometimes intentionally. Only forgiveness can heal these kinds of hurts that tend to destroy relationships. There is a saying that married couples should not go to bed at night angry with each other. Each day the hurts of that day should be forgiven and healed. This is a wise saying that helps marriages survive. Learning to put this saying into practice now with your friends can be a powerful help to a successful marriage later.

Be willing to change. Successful marriage depends on growth. Growth means change. A couple who refuse to grow are doomed to a dying relationship. If you are a flexible, growing person, willing "to roll with the punches" while young, then you'll tend to be open to growth later on.

Learn self-control. Marriage demands discipline, the willingness to sacrifice personal pleasure for the partner and the children. Marriage demands fidelity to the other person, the turning away from temptation to a lifelong commitment of love to the marriage partner. Self-control and fidelity are not "caught," nor do they come easily. They are learned before marriage, while a person is young.

The real test of a growing self-discipline is how before marriage you treat your own sexuality and that of your friends. Sex is a great gift from God: It is beautiful and sacred. Sexual intercourse—as the symbol of total sharing between man and woman—expresses a total commitment and giving to the other. This kind of total commitment—with no conditions attached—can truly be expressed only in marriage. By struggling with the sexual temptations that will naturally come along, you can learn the kind of self-discipline that is a great help in preserving fidelity after marriage.

MORE CRITERIA

1. Add at least one more suggestion to the list given above. First, though, discuss the list with a "happily married" couple. Write a short paragraph for your suggestion. Share these with your classmates.

2. Rate yourself on the five items listed above. Use the following numbers:

   4—this describes me very well
   3—this is me most of the time
   2—this is me some of the time
   1—I need work on this item

   _____ a. Am able to cultivate friendships

   _____ b. Can communicate

   _____ c. Can forgive

   _____ d. Am willing to change

   _____ e. Am self-controlled

3. Discuss these questions after you have thought them through for yourself.

   a. What does *fidelity* in a relationship mean?

   b. What does it mean to say marriage is a *permanent* and *exclusive* relationship?

   c. What do you mean by a *total* commitment?

SUMMARY

1. Marriage is a special sign, a sacrament of God's love. It says that God loves men and women the way they are and that he blesses their life together in a special, unique way.

2. Marital love is a sign of God's love for us. Jesus is present to the couple to help them live their daily life. The Spirit enters their hearts to sustain them in their commitment to each other. Children are a tremendous symbol of divine love which is made manifest in marriage.

3. Our Lord sanctified marriage by restoring its permanency and elevating the position of women. The great theologians through the ages always maintained that marriage is a sacrament.

4. Christian marriage has two purposes: the mutual sharing and growth in grace and love between husband and wife and the procreation and education of children.

5. Marriage as covenant—an open-ended, 100 percent commitment to love and be faithful to the other partner—is a rich biblical way to image Christian marriage. Seen this way, marriage is in miniature a symbol of God's love in Jesus Christ for his people, the church.

6. Successful marriage demands preparation. Among other factors, here are a few that will help prepare a person for married life with a spouse: cultivate friendships, learn communication skills, learn to forgive, be willing to change, and learn self-control.

EVALUATION

Suppose your pastor invited you to give a short talk to an engaged couple about to get married. Based on what you have learned in this chapter, make an outline for that talk. Include in it the five most important things you think should be said about Christian marriage.

OTHER RESEARCH ASSIGNMENTS

A. Divorce. A short chapter like this simply cannot treat all the topics that really ought to be treated on the subject of marriage. The chapter highlighted the theology of marriage and looked at the ideal of Christian marriage. But, as we all know, sometimes marriages fail. Research some of the following themes by using the *Catholic Periodical and Literature Index* (to locate relevant articles) and some recent books on the topics:

1. Reasons marriages fail

2. Church teaching on separation and divorce

3. Church teaching on divorce and remarriage

4. Church ministry to the divorced and separated

B. Birth Control. Another topic not treated in this chapter is birth control. You might wish to read Pope Paul VI's famous *Humanae Vitae* (*Of Human Life*) which clearly presents church teaching on this issue. Or check one of the standard catechisms to see what are acceptable methods of family limitation for Catholic couples. Here are a few suggestions: *Christ Among Us* by Anthony Wilhelm (Paulist Press, 1975), *The Teaching of Christ* (Our Sunday Visitor Press, 1976), *An American Catholic Catechism* (The Seabury Press, 1975) or *The Catholic Catechism* by John Hardon, S.J. (Doubleday & Company, Inc., 1975). You may wish to read the entry in the *New Catholic Encyclopedia,* too. All of these are good sources for research on a variety of topics. They all include a major section on the sacraments. Another superb reference for your research topics is Fr. Richard McBrien's *Catholicism* (Winston Press, 1980). His chapters on the sacraments are excellent.

C. Biography of a Marriage. Interview an older couple, preferably your grandparents (if they are alive), about their marriage. Write a short biography about their marriage together and discuss why it has been a successful one. You may want to present them with a copy of your work. Share it with the class, too.

D. Report Options. Make a report on one of the following:

1. Engaged Encounters or Marriage Encounters

2. Programs in your parish and the diocese for engaged and married couples

10

Conclusion—
Some Reflections and a Review

You must worship the Lord your God,
and serve him alone.

—Mt 4:10

You have made it to the last chapter! Congratulations and thank you for your serious study of the sacraments. This brief final chapter will attempt to do three things: (1) Discuss, in question-and-answer format, a few questions that have not been covered earlier but which are often raised when the sacraments are studied. (2) Present one concluding exercise so that you can apply some of the concepts you have learned in this book. (3) Give a short quiz to test your understanding of the book. At the end of the quiz, the pages on which the correct answers can be found will be given.

A FEW QUESTIONS

1. Are the sacraments a form of prayer? Most definitely the sacraments are prayer! The sacraments are known as *liturgical* prayer. Let's take the Eucharist as an example. In the Eucharist, the Christian community gathers together to *adore* (worship) the Father through Jesus. In addition, the community *thanks* God for what he has accomplished in the Lord. (Recall that *Eucharist*

257

means thanksgiving.) Remember, too, that in the eucharistic liturgy we ask God to forgive us our sins as we *express sorrow* for our past offenses. Finally, at the Mass we *petition* God for many favors, both for the community and for ourselves.

Traditionally, prayer has been defined as "the raising of the mind and heart to God." This is precisely what we do in all the sacraments. Prayer has also been divided into four categories, according to the reasons or purposes for which we pray: adoration (worship), thanksgiving, contrition (expression of sorrow) and petition (asking for something). The Eucharist is an excellent example of how all four of these come together in one sacrament. (As an exercise, decide what categories of prayer are present in each of the other sacraments.)

2. You have used the term "liturgy." What exactly is meant by that? *Liturgy* is the public worship of God which the Christian community does in union with Jesus. The term comes from a Greek word which means "the people's work." One of the tasks of the Christian community is to worship the Father. It does this through the liturgy—rituals like the sacraments, the official prayer of the church called the Divine Office (recited daily by priests) and special blessings for certain occasions like the blessing of a new church building. The liturgy is primarily addressed to the Father in union with Jesus and the Spirit.

Another way to describe liturgical prayer is to distinguish it from private prayer. The liturgy is the *official public* worship our religious community as a group offers to God. Christian liturgy is the *celebration* of the Father's saving actions in Jesus Christ.

3. What about worship? Worship is something that people in every religion do. It is a prayerful acknowledgment of God's greatness. It is the highest form of liturgical prayer. It expresses to God that he is supreme and that we humans are gratefully dependent on him. Christians worship God out of loving praise rather than terrifying fear because Jesus tells us that God is a loving Father. "Loving God above all things" implies that we will thankfully and humbly adore him.

When the Christian community gathers publicly to worship God our Father we are telling the world something. We are telling the world that we love and honor God. We are telling others that we love and honor God by gathering as a family, a community of love which every man, woman and child is invited to join. By gathering together, we are reminding ourselves and telling the world that we are publicly dedicating ourselves to live as the Father's children and serve not only each other but all people, too.

4. What are "sacramentals"? A sacramental is (1) a prayer of the church requesting our Lord's blessing for someone or something, or (2) the object which is blessed. Some of the most common sacramentals include blessed candles and pictures, medals and scapulars, statues, the rosary, the stations of the cross, holy water, benediction of the Blessed Sacrament and the Divine Office recited by priests.

When we use sacramentals we should have a couple of attitudes. First, we should use them reverently. When we use them with devotion and faith we are petitioning our Lord to help us in some way. Our Lord himself asked that we pray often for the things we need (Lk 11:1-13). Second, we should avoid superstition. Sacramentals are not magicians' tools that automatically bring about what we want. Rather, they are signs that help us reach out to the Lord. They can and do prepare us for the important signs of our faith—the sacraments—and remind us of our Lord's constant care for us.

5. How are the sacraments depicted in Christian art? Here are some of the more common ways the seven sacraments are depicted in Christian art. You might want to try to find an example of each of these. Or, perhaps for extra credit, your teacher will allow you to make a banner or some other artwork depicting symbolically a given sacrament. Finally, you might research the meaning of these particular symbols.

Baptism — three fishes; streams of water (swimming with fish); font; shell with water

Confirmation — a dove; seven flames in the shape of tongues

Eucharist — a host; wheat and grapes; loaves and fishes; birds and grapes; stag and fountain

Reconciliation — keys

Anointing of the sick — a dove with an olive branch in its beak; lighted candles

Holy orders — a cup or chalice with a host resting on a bible; stole; keys

Marriage — two joined hands with IHS* above them; two interlocking rings

*IHS—the first three letters of the Greek name for Jesus; a monogram for Christ

A FINAL IMPORTANT EXERCISE

You are drawing to the close of your study of the sacraments. It might be good for you to pause here and "pull it all together." Remember one of the definitions of sacrament from Chapter 2: St. Thomas Aquinas defined sacrament as an "efficacious symbol"—a special kind of symbol that effects (causes) what it symbolizes and symbolizes what it causes.

For a final exercise, let's work with this definition. Below is a "sacrament matrix." In the spaces provided, state for each sacrament what the sacrament causes and what it points to or symbolizes. If you complete this matrix rather easily, you have done a commendable job in studying the sacraments. When you are finished with this exercise, compare your answers with those of a classmate. Then, the entire class should compose a single matrix. Use this final matrix as a review for the short quiz that follows. (Note that a few of the blocks are filled in to give you a start on the exercise.)

THE SACRAMENTS	THIS SACRAMENT BRINGS ABOUT THE FOLLOWING:	THIS SACRAMENT SYMBOLIZES
Baptism	• initiation into the Christian community • divine sonship or daughtership (add to this list)	
Confirmation		
Eucharist		• unity with the Lord and Christian community (add to this)
Reconciliation		• forgiveness (add to this)
Anointing of the sick	• physical healing (add to this)	
Holy orders		
Marriage		

Short Quiz on the Book

Directions:

Try your hand at these questions to review some of the concepts you learned from this book. To check your answers, reread those pages indicated at the end of the quiz. Your teacher can also help with the right responses. Good luck!

For multiple-choice items, pick the *best* choice.

_____ 1. *Viaticum* is another term for:

a. the anointing of the confirmed; b. Holy Communion given to the dying; c. penance administered by the priest; d. the rite of ordination of a bishop.

_____ 2. Holy orders ordains the following as special ministers for the church:

a. bishops, priests and deacons only; b. bishops and priests only; c. priests only; d. bishops, priests, deacons and servers.

_____ 3. The sacrament known as the sacrament of Christian maturity is:

a. reconciliation; b. marriage; c. holy orders; d. confirmation.

_____ 4. The Eucharist is important in our lives because:

a. it celebrates meeting other people; b. creates and celebrates the unity among Christians; c. it is a call to support the local church; d. it reminds us to be holy during the week.

_____ 5. When husband and wife love in a Christian marriage they are truly reflecting God's love. (True or false.)

_____ 6. The Father's loving forgiveness is celebrated in:

a. baptism, reconciliation, Eucharist and anointing
b. reconciliation, Eucharist, confirmation and orders
c. matrimony, baptism and holy orders
d. reconciliation, Eucharist, confirmation and anointing

_____ 7. Here are a number of elements which could describe a sacrament.

Choose the letter that *best* describes what a sacrament is:

a. something only a priest does, a sign of grace, shared prayer
b. a sign of a sacred reality, a meeting with the risen Lord, a communal liturgical celebration
c. a means of grace, holy water, bread and wine
d. a priestly blessing, a cause of grace, the church

_____ 8. In the theology of Christian marriage today, the sacrament is best described as:

a. a life of commitment as long as the couple love each other; b. a mutually binding contract of marital rights and duties; c. a covenant of love which is a mutual lifelong commitment of a couple to each other in Christ; d. a meaningful liturgical celebration with lots of social customs.

_____ 9. Which of the following is *not* one of the four parts of the sacrament of reconciliation?

a. initiation into the harmed community; b. confession; c. act of penance (satisfaction); d. contrition; e. absolution

_____ 10. Jesus is the sacrament of the Father. The _____ is the sacrament of Jesus.

_____ 11. The sacrament of reconciliation has undergone considerable change throughout the history of the church. (True or false.)

_____ 12. Baptismal water symbolizes:

a. life; b. death; c. rebirth; d. all of these.

_____ 13. "What God has joined, men must not divide" comes from the liturgy of which sacrament?

a. holy orders; b. marriage; c. confirmation; d. Eucharist; e. reconciliation

_____ 14. The parable of the Prodigal Son refers to which part of Jesus' message?

a. the call to unity; b. the incarnational principle; c. God's forgiveness; d. Jesus as the message.

_____ 15. Because Jesus himself did not marry, in his earthly ministry he probably did not intend marriage to be a Christian sacrament. (True or false.)

_____ 16. In the space provided, write in an acceptable definition of the term *sacrament:*

_____

_____

_____

_____ 17. The description that best fits Eucharist is:

a. it celebrates God's presence in all of created reality;
b. it is the one true sacrament;
c. it is a sacrifice, holy meal and celebration of love
d. it is obedience unto death.

____ 18. The twofold aim of Christian marriage is:

   a. the mutual love and sharing between husband and wife; and

   b. _____

Questions 19-25: Match the value of Jesus (column B) which is exemplified best by a particular sacrament (column A)

A. Sacraments	B. Values of Jesus
____ 19. Baptism	a. healing and strength to endure
____ 20. Confirmation	b. strength of unity to live a life of love
____ 21. Eucharist	c. conversion; accepting the good news
____ 22. Reconciliation	d. ministry of love to spouse and children
____ 23. Anointing of the sick	e. forgiveness and reunion with the community
____ 24. Matrimony	f. ministry of love to God's people
____ 25. Holy orders	g. strength of the Spirit to live a life of committed service

____ 26. Which of the following is *not* true of the sacrament of confirmation?

   a. it initiates us more deeply into the faith community;
   b. it celebrates the gift of the Holy Spirit;
   c. it must be received when a person is psychologically ready;
   d. it is known as the sacrament of witness.

_____ 27. Briefly list three things you can do now to help you prepare for a life of Christian marriage:

a. _____

_____

b. _____

_____

c. _____

_____

_____ 28. The best description of *minister* is:

a. the equivalent of priest; b. a prophet in the Christian community; c. one who is ordained; d. one who serves.

_____ 29. At confirmation the gifts of the Holy Spirit are celebrated. List three of them here and briefly define them or give an example of each.

a. _____

_____

b. _____

_____

c. _____

_____

_____ 30. Another term for the Eucharist is:

a. the Mass; b. agape; c. berakhah; d. all of these.

_____ 31. Briefly discuss two essential qualities of a good priest:

a. _____

_____

b. _____

_____

_____ 32. Jesus taught that sickness and suffering are the results of our own personal sin or the sins of our parents. (True or false.)

_____ 33. Only in recent times has the laity been allowed to handle the consecrated bread and wine. (True or false.)

_____ 34. Which of the following is an effect of the sacrament of the anointing of the sick:

a. it wipes away sin; b. it brings spiritual healing; c. it brings physical healing; d. it strengthens and comforts the sick person during the illness; e. all of these.

_____ 35. The summit of Christian worship is:

a. baptism; b. the Eucharist; c. confirmation; d. holy orders.

ANSWERS: You can find the answers to this quiz on the follow-ing pages:

1. p. 199
2. pp. 214-215
3. p. 97
4. pp. 139-142
5. pp. 234-236
6. pp. 69; 139, 141-142; 157; 197
7. See Chapter 2, especially pp. 41-44; 49-51
8. pp. 244-245
9. pp. 176-177
10. pp. 46-47
11. pp. 169-173
12. pp. 65-70
13. pp. 248-249
14. pp. 20-21

15. p. 240
16. Any definition from pp. 41-42; also, the one on pp. 49-50
17. pp. 131-132; 139-142
18. p. 245
19-25. p. 53
26. pp. 51-55; 97
27. pp. 250-251
28. pp. 207-209
29. p. 104
30. pp. 126-128
31. pp. 217-219
32. p. 191
33. pp. 135-138
34. p. 195
35. p. 142